GREG

may this BOOK SHOW
HOW GOD IS AT WORK
IN THE WORLD.

Rollie

9. 6. 2008

FOR A MOMENT WE HAD *THE WAY*

ROLLAND ROBINSON

The Story of The Way: 1966-1970

A Nearly Forgotten History of a Community Organization
that Almost Turned Minneapolis Upside Down

Andover,
Minnesota

The front cover is composed of a photograph of the Minneapolis Police Department's Fourth Precinct. Overlaid is a sketch of The Way that was originally located at 1913 Plymouth Avenue that is now the site of the police building.

ISBN 13: 978-1-931945-48-9
ISBN 10: 1-931945-48-0

Library of Congress Catalog Number: 2006925289

Printed in the United States of America

First Printing: May 2006

10 09 08 07 06   5 4 3 2 1

Expert Publishing, Inc.
14314 Thrush Street NW,
Andover, MN 55304-3330
Andover,   1-877-755-4966
Minnesota   www.expertpublishinginc.com

This book is dedicated to Syl Davis and Willie Mae Dixon who knew the game, knew all the positions, knew the right moves, knew what the score was, and still played their hearts out. Another wise man that lived through another time of doubt and change wrote daring words. It speaks to the spirit of all those at **The Way** who dared more than most—

> *However mean your life is, meet it, and live it;*
>
> *love your life, poor as it is.*
>
> *Why should we be in such haste to succeed,*
>
> *and in such desperate enterprises?*
>
> *If a man does not keep pace with his companions,*
>
> *perhaps it is because he hears a different drummer.*
>
> *Let him step to the music which he hears,*
>
> *however measured or far away.*
>
> **—Henry Thoreau**[1]

Both Syl and Willie Mae have, as the blues sing it, "gone down the line." Both listened to the music of their souls, the distant drummer's measure of time beating out the steps of freedom.

Contents

Acknowledgements

This book is a collective effort of many people. I am particularly grateful to Barbara Greenwald-Davis, the widow of Syl Davis, who first encouraged me to write this book. I am indebted to my good friends Susan Breedlove, Reverend Karl Johnson, Reverend Ken Beck, Reverend Charles Grose, and Karen Nasby for reading early drafts and making helpful suggestions. My good editors, Harry and Sharron Stockhausen, deserve special thanks. First, for recognizing the publishable value of the book and secondly, for their strong editorial persistence in making it a better book.

I want to offer a special thank you to Sage Cowles, Penny Winton, and Louise McCannel who were there at **The Way** in those early years and saw their way to give of their resources so this book could be published. I would add a thank you to David and Karen Nasby and my three children, Jonathan, Stephen, and Kristin, who also contributed toward the publication of this book.

Alice, my wife, has patiently listened to me through the various stages of this book and always brought a smile of encouragement when it was most needed.

Mahmoud El-Kati and Louise McCannel played key roles at **The Way**. These two persons have spent their entire lives committed to the struggle of justice. The courage of their convictions is wedded to a wisdom that comes through their writings. I have quoted extensively from their work as well as benefited from their wisdom.

The book makes use of the term "Other" that may be new to the reader. However it has a long practice. The philosopher Jean-Paul Sartre wrote a philosophical biography *Saint Genet* on the writer and criminal Jean Genet. Sartre makes the point that Genet, being a thief, is the Other, other than the law-abiding citizen. The Other is the evildoer, thus making the law abiding person look good. Good looks at its twin and calls the image evil. This exercise is a modern version of the scapegoat ceremony and, like the ancient practice, makes for a clear conscience. The Other is explored in the chapter "The Way and Ishmael."

The chapter "A Way of Writing" is indebted to Edward Said and his reflections on the use of the essay form in his book *Reflections on Exile*. The writer Ralph Ellison inspired the title "The Way of Telling The Story Right: The Unlikeness of a Documentary Or Leaving Sociology to the Scientists." "The Way and Ishmael" utilizes the insights of Franz Fanon's *Black Skins, White Masks*. Walter Wink's *Naming the Powers* is key to the chapter "The Way and Minneapolis." Joseph Washington's book *Black Sects and Cults* contributed to the reigning insight of the chapter on "The Way and the Black Church." "The Way and Black Power" chapter is indebted to Stokely Carmichael and Charles V. Hamilton's book *Black Power: The Politics of Liberation in America* and Dr. Martin Luther King's, Jr. last book, *Where Do We Go From Here: Community or Chaos?*

"The Way Toward Inclusive Education" utilizes the work of two authors. The first is Peter L. Berger's *The Sacred Canopy*. The second is Paulo's Freire's *Pedagogy of the Oppressed*. *The Covenanted Self* by Walter Brueggemann influenced my thinking for the chapter "The Way Toward Restorative Justice." "The Way Toward Renewal of Public Life" utilizes the insights from *The Company of Strangers* by Parker J. Palmer.

Such is the collective effort in the making of *For A Moment We Had The Way*. I am indebted to this company of wordsmiths whose abiding witness carries on Thomas Kydd's maximum, "When words no longer prevail, violence prevails."

January 16, 2006

Seventy-seventh Anniversary of The Birth of
Dr. Martin Luther King, Jr.

Preface

Several persons, who in their youth were influenced in their life direction by being part of the early days of **The Way**, came together in late 1997 in the home of Barbara Greenwald-Davis, the widow of Syl Davis. Syl was the first director of **The Way** during its early innovative and controversial years. They were saddened at what was happening. Another generation had been born that never heard of **The Way**. They recognized that a key part of their history, as well as the history of the community, was being forgotten, written off by not being written down, not being retold and recorded. This small group decided to create a documentary of **The Way**. They began to collect newspaper clippings, identify persons who still lived in the community who were on the staff or on its board or, like themselves, came to **The Way**. It was then that I was contacted, for I had served on **The Way** board since its beginning in 1966 and six months later was elected board president serving in that position until the end of 1970. It turned out I had kept a large file of documents from those early years.

I agreed to help. It was only after discovering Louise McCannel's, who once referred to herself as "the historian of **The Way**,"[1] archives now in the custodial care of the Minnesota Historical Society, I knew I had serious work ahead of me. Going through Louise's archives, along with my own files, I found things dramatically changed following the resignation of Syl Davis in late 1970. With Syl's departure, the extraordinary challenge and subversive witness emblematic of **The Way** changed. It took on the character of a more conventional social agency soon to become dependent on monies from the United Way. The new leadership sought to disenfranchise itself from its immediate past by calling the organization **The New Way.** That was reason enough to focus on the years 1966 to 1970 when Syl Davis was the director of **The Way**.

Things started to prove interesting once the decision was made that a wall of history on **The Way** would be our starting point. As the wall of history began to take on an outline, as the story began to shape itself, persons in the group began to express feelings that a documentary was not the way to record this history, at least not initially. Too much was involved. Besides, raising money for a one-hour documentary would be beyond the resources the group could raise. There was also the feeling that a documentary would leave too much unsaid and that a book could be a more reliable witness. So we come to the writing of this book.

ONE

AUTHOR'S INTRODUCTION

Older souls, no matter their age,
have made my soul wiser,
spoke of what we thought,
told us of what we knew,
that gave us each leave
to be what we are, truly.

—Rolland Robinson[1]

A Way Of Writing

Some have relied on what they knew;
Others on being simply true.
What worked for them might work for you.
No memory of having starred
Atones for later disregard
Or keeps the end from being hard.

—Robert Frost [1]

Perspective

One must declare oneself sooner or later. I have decided sooner to be the better course, to declare my intention up front, offer the perspective of my choice of materials to help you, the reader, find your way through the unfolding narrative that continually shifts the shape of this book. Unfolding is tricky. You can fold a sheet of paper into a boat, taught to us as children, to have it unfold back into a blank sheet of paper, leaving the creases of its former self behind. You hold the paper in your hand, press it to your chest knowing it once was a boat. The semblance and the assembling intertwined in your imagination have made you alive to the possibilities that there is more here than meets the eye. I encourage you as the reader to unfold the pages of this book to imagine here the creases that interpretation seeks to trace upon the blankness of what only a moment ago was unknown.

To put it plainly, this book is subversive as it offers an alternative way of seeing the world. There is a cry in the world, the cry of the dispossessed, a cry that cannot be stilled. The cry was first heard in a brickyard in ancient Egypt, a cry of slaves for deliverance, and God heard that cry, knew the suffering in that cry, and delivered them from bondage. So this book is subversive in the same unsettling sense. It seeks to give voice to those who live nearly off the page of history on its margins, a voice that is only heard between the lines of recorded history.

There is a story that took place in Jim Crow South told years later by Dr. Howard Thurman, chaplain to the divine at Boston Chapel. It is a subversive story, subversive for it offered an alternative way to speak, to cry out. It is the way of the dispossessed when silenced by authorities.

The story begins with a police killing of a blind African-American. The killing aroused strong feelings in a nameless southern city. The African-American preacher was told by the authorities there would be no sermon at the funeral. The police feared a riot. The funeral was held with police standing in the aisles of the church. The minister didn't give a sermon, as he had been told, but that didn't keep him from praying. The clergyman could have been arrested for speaking to the people but he couldn't be arrested for speaking to God. In his prayer the minister told God everything that happened as the people listened in. Shameful, sordid business, yet it is the way the weak have survived through the years.[2]

I trust the unfolding narrative of *For A Moment We Had The Way* will put you off your guard, act as a destabilizing presence, if only to hear its story on its own terms. It is a story of a group of people that gave vision and heart and feet to an organization known as **The Way** who nearly turned Minneapolis upside down.

The Essay

For A Moment We Had The Way is a book of essays. The essay is accused of being an anachronism, out of date, no longer useful, according to philosopher Theodore Adorno.[3] The essay is a form that places emphasis on incompleteness, a narrative that does not bring closure and conclusion to the current state of affairs. It is precisely the incompleteness of the essay that best suits my purpose. The essay affords the author opportunity to experiment at writing personal reflections on a variety of topics. In that light, anachronism is a good thing, a worthwhile pursuit offering an opening, a clearing for new possibilities. The use of the essay is a stratagem that opens up congealed spaces and so encourages careful interpretation and ingenious speculation. It is not the intent of this approach to recapture a time gone by but rather to signify a congruence of our present hour to the struggle of another hour. So these essays will seek to hear again the indestructible words and gestures that are nearly forgotten under the dulling context of time and intentional forgetfulness.

The vocabulary of these essays will be philosophical and theological, for both disciplines recognize the long-standing belief that no hard definition in this world can capture what both the philosopher and the theologian would call "Spirit" that is continually afoot and will not die. Such a Spirit informs freedom and justice that comes only with struggle in a world where the preponderance of power necessary to organize human society and establish justice has from times immemorial generated injustice.

Taking A Read On The Way

Doubling Back: Mapping By Memory

Henry Gates, African-American writer and scholar, tells how Charlie Parker practiced playing new chords. He would play a chord on his alto saxophone then repeat it before reversing the same chord to hear if he understood correctly what he had just played. The past is seldom past except to historians and those who live from one day to another lost in the amnesia of the present. Yet there is always more to the present than what appears. In certain ways the past lives on in forms of remembrance that are quickened by a word, a song, a taste of ice cream, or the memory of mama's dress.

Alex Haley remembered. He would not forget. He traced his "Roots" in a speaking book that later became a ground breaking television program of his African ancestors, their passage in a hell hole on a slave ship, their cruel and barbaric enslavement through generations of plantation masters in the American South, to their emancipation and struggle for freedom their descendents have yet to win.

When Alex Haley interviewed Malcolm X for what would become the book *Autobiography of Malcolm X,* he could not get Malcolm to talk about himself. This articulate man only spoke of his faith and

Elijah Muhammad, the spiritual leader of the Black Muslim Nation. Haley insisted he already had written articles on Malcom X's faith; now he needed to write a book on his life. Still Malcolm did not say anything about himself. Suddenly, it came to Alex Haley to ask Malcolm if there was anything about his mother he remembered. At that moment, Malcolm seemed suspended in mid-air, remembering his mother. He began to talk as if with another voice about his mother's old and torn dress she wore as she bent over a stove making a meal from little of nothing.

This is how Malcom X's biography started to write itself that night he remembered his mother. Pacing the floor, Malcom had all he could do to catch in the net of his memory the scenes that brought him back to "Red," the street wise guy, strong and able to deal with the threats, full of gangster shows that led him to prison and beyond—to the teachings of Elijah Muhammad. But it was his mama's dress that brought back his life.

The story of Malcom X remembering his mother shows how the past works on us and often through us, opening doors to the future through remembrance. This book is part history and part biography seeking to recount backwards the life and times of a community organization known simply as **The Way**.

Time's incessant demand made a wilderness of our experience. We lived through the mid-sixties into the early seventies on fast forward. So many things happened at speeds beyond our imagining and outside the frame of our usual understanding.

This book of memory seeks to place in slow motion the dance and beat of those days and how they account for much that is going on in human relations in the Twin Cities and beyond today.

The Way could be re-imaged like a work of art, a riff on expectant hopes, and the soundings on the tragedies of loss; whereas, this book is much less, though done in full consciousness, seeking to give meaning to those hopes and tragedies as they were lived out in people's lives. This writer still lives in both times. In the latter time of the present, he seeks to show how events appear to repeat those of an earlier hour. These two times are quite different worlds but close enough that one can walk between them.

This approach influences the way you, as the reader, will interpret what you read, how you take a read on what is being said. This writer believes that no matter what your allegiance or views, you will find this story is your story as well. As this book remembers **The Way** and the people who were part of its story, so **The Way's** spirit will touch you. **The Way's** spirit is still alive to shape the struggle of those who seek to be free of poverty and racial injustice. It is in this spirit I pass on to the next generation these gifts of remembrance, the stories of struggle that make us human.

A Book of Memory Remembering

Why do people remember? What does a community need to remember to continue being a vibrant community? We know that when a community no longer remembers, reassembles its events and biography of its members, it dies.

There is the voluntary memory that would, as the historian, bring back the related events of a bygone era. As it was for the French writer Proust, such memory is nearly useless. The voluntary memory we refer to is the memory of the conventional historian who is content with the official record of events. I have come to know that the official historical record of the past forty years of Minneapolis' Near North Side is stilted and outrageously contrived. It is not the story of the people who lived there and suffered there and died there.

There is another kind of memory, more involuntary, nearly secretive. It comes to the surface through the association of a place, a smell, the voice of one now gone. It is the memory embodied in the body of one who lived in those times. So I have reflected upon the measure of change and understanding that has come to me of those years. That is why it is so important to remember what will never appear in text books, to remember what cannot finally be pinned down into definitions and slogans, to remember the people who struggled and bore witness to a greater dignity toward which we still aspire.

At the turn of the new millennium, those in the Jewish community who had left in the sixties wrote a book, *North Side Memories*,[1] that would stand alongside a documentary video created in order that subsequent generations would remember the Jewish sojourn in North Minneapolis. Remembering was not always done this way for the Jewish community. Only after the erosion of traditional ways of liturgy and story did the historian become necessary and that not until the nineteenth century. Increasingly so, we have all become like the wicked son in the Passover Seder who says, "your story, not mine." So we write a book about memory and remembering, a book open to the past and to the future, a book that listens to those who have died so it can find the words and stories to speak to those yet to be born.

The Way Of Telling
The Story Right:

The Unlikeliness of A Documentary or Leaving Sociology to The Scientists

Talk About The Way

The outrageous title of this essay are the magical words of Ralph Ellison.[1] This powerful writer sought to savor the richness of African-American speech. It is speech ever recreating itself and so evading the slow death of habitual overuse. The idiomatic expressions and rhetorical flourishes that leave the sociologist curiously cold is the fruit basket upset that catches the artist's imagination. Here reality is brightly displayed in magical form revealing the endless ways truth shows itself in the human condition. This is how this essay seeks to capture the talk about **The Way**.

People will always talk about **The Way**.[2] If not the historical one, then certainly the one that continually shapes their hopes and dreams. The disenfranchised will always create organizations like **The Way** because it is the way they seek a voice, if not to change others, certainly to keep themselves from being changed.

The Way that lived and had its being on the Near North Side of Minneapolis is no more. Another organization claimed its building but not its name. When **The Way**, in its early and formative years, stood its ground against incredible odds, people who talked about

The Way were fascinated by **The Way,** angered by **The Way,** bewildered by **The Way,** and, at times, even embarrassed by **The Way.** Yet the one thing people never did was to disown **The Way,** not by people who knew they did not have justice in the criminal justice system, not by people who knew they did not have an equal share in the economics of the wealthiest nation on the earth.

The Way was always more than its historical self. **The Way** could never be simply isolated and identified. **The Way** would never be that easily available to those who would have liked to reduplicate it or make it disappear. Yet **The Way** will never completely disappear because it is part of the ongoing struggle for dignity and equal justice—a struggle caught in people's stories. If ever a documentary is made of the voices who have stories to tell, then you will realize **The Way** was more than another organization. **The Way** held the promise and hope for a better life for people who had been trampled on far too many times. The stories will be disconcerting as they are discerning of a struggle about the truth, the truth about this society, the truth about ourselves. This truth is about how life is with those who suffer unjustly, something not known precisely until it is precisely given over to telling and articulation. These stories invite you to leave your bias at the door, taking off your shoes of expectation. If you do, you will get an ear full of the truth that is as much about you as it is of the teller.

The story of **The Way** is larger than life but never larger than the truth. There will be something about these stories that is a bit unsure, inscrutable. There is no inside story on **The Way** unless one goes inside oneself. There is no final secret of disclosure about **The Way** that will yield new truth. Those who look for such things always come up empty handed. But those who seek a greater truth will find there is something for them in **The Way's** story.

Seeking To Be a Serious Storyteller and a Reliable Witness

I have come to the task of writing this book with the imaginative wherewithal of a storyteller seeking to catch the tenor and tone, as well as the style and wit, of those storytellers back in the sixties, mid-wives at the birth of **The Way**. What many others have discarded as worthless I have assembled in a poetic way with a surety that will not be easily dismissed by the current regime of historians and other caretakers of our memory. I have sought to present the other-ness of the past with its obstinate unfamiliarity, following the routes of illumination in working against type, in waylaying the present by the past as to show the thinness of the line of certainty upon which we stand, for our forebearers shoulders are beneath our feet.

TWO

PART BIOGRAPHY, PART FICTION

Biography is the art of concealment;
fiction is that of revelation.

—Peter Ackroyd[1]

Syl Davis

Syl Davis grew up there.
He grew up on the North Side.
And, like many who live there,
Syl was wise.
He knew things do not change,
only we do.
Like his elders, Syl knew you can get rid of your clothes
but never your thoughts.

Growing and wising up came to Syl
seeing the world from the other side.
North Side is the underside of Minneapolis.
You can see downtown from there,
though making it downtown is another matter.
The distance from there to downtown
is more than a lifetime away.
Not that folks want to make it downtown.
However, the temptation is cast in one's direction—

"One would be a fool if you didn't want to make it."
Making it and being a fool has something to do with downtown.

North Side is like no other place in the city,
a place feared by those who live elsewhere.
The North Side frontier is paroled by police
and barracked by schools where respect
for a system designed from elsewhere is taught.
North Side is the place where people
who went to school elsewhere
come to visit or work carrying the credentials
of social scientist and social worker,
parole officer and teacher,
all agents of the government.
They hide their dominion even though they harbor sympathies
that betray the system they represent;
still they come to take up practice as upholders of good order—
an order whose invisible hands make connections
running half way around the world
to peddle cocaine to North Side's very doorstep.
North Minneapolis is alive in the minds of those who live elsewhere,
a place of crime,
a place where criminals hang out,
for the criminals have no place to live, always on the run.
North Side is a neighborhood that lives off
the negative cash flow of prostitution and shoplifting
and where the young disappear
to spend a lifetime behind bars.

Syl stood in there
that night in August 1966
when Plymouth Avenue took fire
as rage and anger burned to high heaven.
An older generation sat on their porches
looking on with a critical patience

borne out of a struggle that carried the scars
of too many broken promises.
Not Syl. He stood in there for the young people
who ripped up a bit of Plymouth rock
and heaved it toward downtown.
Some thought hell broke loose,
while others thought liberation arrived.
Syl Davis stood in there on a night
misconstrued and misunderstood
by nearly everyone involved.
Yet out of this confusion
something important came—
a community organization known as **The Way.**

Fortune favors audacity and youth.
Never be wise with the foolish
and never be foolish with the wise
and notice men's moods for they tell you much.

—Syl Davis[1]

Syl Davis possessed a grasp of larger issues.

On December 1,1968, the *Minneapolis Tribune*
devoted the "Sunday Magazine" to **The Way**.
An apocalyptic image of catastrophe
appeared on the front cover
displaying a photograph with a Black hand holding a string
to a ticking clock moments away from midnight.
Midnight held either the end of something
or the beginning of something.
The *Tribune* offered
a provocative and compelling image of **The Way.**
Syl could read people as well as the signs of the times.
Syl knew what worked and what didn't.
He worked at Wells Settlement House on the North Side.
Syl resonated to the philosophy of advocacy

of the settlement house movement
started by Jane Addams in the later part of the nineteenth century.
Sadly, it descendents squired its advocacy approach
downward toward servicing the poor.
Syl never accepted the settlement house definition for **The Way.**
What good would another community service center do
for troubled kids if they were never told the truth—
that their future is in jeopardy.
Pressure to take care of troublesome kids
by getting them off the street and out of trouble
is what the "powers to be" wanted.
The Way did not take direction from downtown,
rather **The Way** directed people
toward their own empowerment.
Syl Davis boldly said,
"The North Side didn't need more services.
People need to be enfranchised
and given the opportunity to create and run their own institutions."

Syl Davis built his entire life around conflict.

He gained wisdom in knowing there are no safe places.
He held to the truth of an old proverb:
"A wise man is mightier than a strong man
and a man of knowledge than the man who has strength." [2]
Syl's held to this sense of reality never letting go.
He never let up
even when he desired a season of equilibrium,
a time to gain some safe balance in his own life.
Equilibrium is one thing Syl never found.

Syl Davis tilted toward seeking the truth.

He could hide from the truth
but not for long.
The truth is always too persuasive.
Syl believed unless one saw the truth about oneself,

one could never be free.
This is the source of his indictment on elected leaders
as well as on the many self-anointed community leaders
who continued to show up behind some cause.
To be a leader one must be just
and to be just one has to know the truth about oneself,
and be true to it.
In this, Syl Davis lived a free man, beholden to none.

*The search for truth is not given
to every man; for the truth is hidden
under many lies and can only be
found in the depths.*

—Syl Davis [3]

Power did not beguile Syl Davis.

In the early heady days of **The Way**
some suggested Syl should run for public office.
He didn't and for good reason.
Syl knew the value of power
and, if left to its own ends, power could destroy one.
He saw too much of power's wrongful use
not to know the temptation of power.
Power became the drug for the powerless,
the way out from under the rule of others.
Power can be a temptation to violence.
What becomes of power without force?
More, what becomes of power without justice?
Syl Davis understood the alchemy of these things.

Syl Davis knew more than most.

He heard in the cry of Black Power
a psychological reaction
to the indoctrination that led to the perfect slave.
The new sense of manhood, person-hood,

that arose in that cry
signaled the death throe of an old racist system.
The clock about to strike midnight
on the front cover of the *Tribune* feature issue on **The Way**
is more prophetic than the writers realized.

Syl Davis was rhetorical and secretive, passionate yet oblique.

Syl was sly.
He possessed a cunning that made some distrust him.
Syl knew without cunning life was reduced
to the narrowest forms of control.
Mother wit was a gift given to Syl
by his ancestors and mentors
who knew in their bones the terror of slavery
as well as the beguiling temptations of life.
To protect one's life,
one is forced to look beneath appearances,
to take nothing for granted,
to hear the meaning behind words,
to watch the intention that backs up promises,
to survive the worst that life throws at one—
such are the combative ways one ceases to be controlled by fear.

Syl Davis did not make things simple.

People want things simple.
Syl thought better of people.
He knew they could do better
than simply carry the burden of their lives.
People are capable of carrying out
a noble enterprise, once they discover
the burden of reality that accompanies such an enterprise.
Reality is not to be avoided or made simple
but to be the very challenge toward greatness.

To be useful is to be doubly useful.

—Syl Davis [4]

Syl Davis took courage to change himself.

Life does not go on continually,
there is discontinuity.
Syl Davis knew that,
experienced it throughout his life, and learned from it.
His own life marked a journey
full of endings and new beginnings.
Syl grieved the closing of **The Way** in 1984.
He felt deep loss in the failure
to reopen **The Way** and keep its name in 1989.
He understood things don't change,
we change.
Syl took courage to change himself,
to accept without bitterness a change
that would lead to a renewal of his own spirit.

"I play for keeps, for things do not keep forever."

—Syl Davis [5]

Syl navigated
the difficult waters of his own latter day passage
not only for his sake,
but for the sake of those who would come after.
Syl Davis found the way.

Willie Mae Dixon

The truth shall make you free.

—John 8:32, RSV
Willie Mae's favorite verse of scripture.

It can be said of Willie Mae Dixon
what Harriet Tubman declared about herself:
"Ain't I some woman!"
True.
Willie Mae was some woman!

She knew suffering caused by the violence of oppressors.
She never forgot it.
More. She used suffering
by turning two events (that I know of)
into powerful weapons to break oppression
that still stalks and kills.

The first event of violence that was forged
into Willie Mae's memory
was the killing death of her niece.
Her niece was one of the children killed
by the terror-bombing of a Sunday School class
in Birmingham, Alabama, in 1963.

The last of the bombers was finally sentenced
nearly forty years later.
Justice's petty pace ironically kept this terrifying act
in the consciousness and conscience
of those who would otherwise have forgotten.
Willie Mae would never forget.

She knew the evil force that killed her niece
still reigned down terror in subtle ways
on the lives of other brothers and sisters.
She would resist.
She would not give up.

The second act of violence that visited her
came the day her father was shot in the back by a
White police officer
in Birmingham, Alabama.
(The officer was later cleared of all charges,
exonerated by the terrifying rubric called justifiable homicide.)
A civil rights demonstration was going on in the city.
Mr. Dixon was about to join it.
He was told by a police officer not to cross the street.
Mr. Dixon said he was simply exercising his constitutional right
to assemble peaceably with his people.
He then turned and walked across the street.
The officer told him, "'Boy, stop or I will shoot."
Mr. Dixon didn't answer to "boy" and kept on walking.
Willie Mae's father was shot because he refused to obey the officer.
It is the road to freedom, the struggle that brings suffering.

Willie Mae never forgot.
Her father's death ran blood red in her thoughts.
Yet she refused vengeance's insistence.
This was one of the amazing facts about Willie Mae Dixon.
She had every reason to strike back in hatred.
She chose not to.
Rather she sought to bring understanding
where there was ignorance,
to bring peace
where there was violence.
She sought to bring a human face to African-American males
and so help them to remove the disfigurement of hatred.

I asked her, "How do you do it?"
Willie Mae said, "My mother taught me
without the cross there ain't no crown."

I asked her that question after she had taken in a young man
to detox him off drugs. She sweated it out with him
in her home for three nights and three days.
Finally, he had fallen asleep.

She decided to leave only to get groceries.
While she was away
he awoke and, seeing Willie Mae was gone,
called a friend to bring a truck.
The two loaded up most of her furniture
and stereo equipment and what valuables
they could get their hands on
and drove off to sell everything for more drugs.
She came back to a nearly empty house.
I asked her why she did not call the police.
She said, "They'll only put him away
for another twenty years.
That's no answer."
Later, when this same young man got in trouble,
it was Willie Mae who was the first person to help.

Willie Mae Dixon was a leading light,
along with Syl Davis,
behind **The Way's** innovative programs
that sought to work with African-Americans
caught in the criminal justice system.

The Way was a creative alternative
that would seek the help of persons
who were born into the same environment as the offenders.
It would begin to break down the wall of hostility
that existed between those in the African-American community
and those representing the system.

Willie Mae knew such programs were needed
from her own experience in working with the courts.
There was the incident where a mother and eleven children
had just arrived in Minneapolis from Mississippi.
The Welfare Department handled them indifferently,
devoid of human compassion and decency.
The mother was told that the best
that could be done for her and her children
was to give them bus fare back to Mississippi.
She had come to Minnesota because she was told
people there would treat her
with more compassion and understanding
than she received in Mississippi.
She could not go back.
She was to appear before a judge.

That was when Willie Mae stepped in.
When she did, it was a sorry day for the Welfare Department.
Willie Mae found an apartment with five bedrooms,
furniture, and food for the family of twelve
in one day.
What the Welfare Department couldn't do—

save offer a bus ticket back to where the family had come from—
Willie Mae had done because of her connections in the community.

Willie Mae knew how to deal with the judge
who was determining the case,
even if it meant embarrassing the Welfare Department
with the truth in court.
She was prepared to risk herself for this family.
When someone connected to the Welfare Department
threatened her with jail,
Willie Mae told the person that there was a cell
with her name on top of it.
She and the mother, along with eleven children,
would go to jail
before Willie Mae would let the family be sent back to Mississippi.
The family stayed in Minnesota.

Working at **The Way** and with the courts
were the beginnings of her advocacy work.
Willie Mae continued her advocacy for people
at the Legal Rights Center.
Willie Mae's Dixon's work led the way
for much of the para-professional legal advocacy
that is done today.

Willie Mae Dixon was seldom given credit.
She never sought it.
She was more concerned for justice than glory;
that would come later,
as it did in 1978 when Willie Mae died.
She was only forty years old.
A victim of cancer
yet a victor over the spiritual disease of despair
that afflicts and can defeat the soul.
The truth had set her free.

THREE

A NEARLY FORGOTTEN HISTORY

Life must be lived forward,
but can only be understood backwards.

—Soren Kierkegaard[1]

Part One:
Trying To Find The Way

Getting Orientated: Plymouth Avenue

To those who never lived in Minneapolis, Plymouth Avenue is main street on the Near North Side. Plymouth Avenue runs east and west bordered on the east by the Mississippi River and to the west by the Minneapolis city limits. There is a business district to the north that runs the length of Broadway as the community is bordered on the south by Bryn Mawr.

Like its namesake Plymouth Colony, Plymouth Avenue continues to symbolize something vital to this nation's origins. Plymouth Colony was settled by Pilgrims professing a belief contrary to the Church of England. King James I, in an epoch-making decision, promised these dissenters could live in freedom, free from restraint. Plymouth Avenue signifies in the minds of some freedom's lasting tradition. It is here we can get our bearings.

You can Judge a Community by Its Façade:
Looking for The Way

Dr. David Taylor, Dean of the General College, University of Minnesota, was quoted in *The Spokesman-Recorder* newspaper that African-American communities do not preserve, as they need to, physical structures that once played a role in their histories. Dr. Taylor made the observation that buildings, once housing important organizations and institutions key to African-American history, need to be preserved. In many cases, he said, there are not even photographs. However, there are first-hand testimonies and these need to be recorded.[1]

If you go looking for **The Way** today you will find it is not there. However, if you know what you are looking for as you drive down Plymouth Avenue, a thanatographical moment can be had. If you have eyes to see beyond appearances, Thanatos, the old Greek word for death, can be found throughout the city and certainly can be found on the Near North Side of Minneapolis. The neighborhood gives witness to the dead, a testimonial to what is not seen.

Let us travel through the customary world of optics and take note of what we see. I ask you to use your mind's eye to observe two prominent buildings that serve as bookends for the community. On the corner of Plymouth and Penn, as you travel east, you can see the Urban League's new building named after two former directors of the Urban League of Minneapolis–Gleason Glover and Gary Sudduth. The building serves as a monument that secures the memory of these persons who were community leaders, advocates for better education and better jobs for minorities, as well as a more just treatment for African-Americans caught in the criminal justice system. This bookend on Plymouth Avenue represents the advocates for *social change*. Traveling further east you will pass a large building on Plymouth and Logan. It is the Fourth Precinct Police Station that takes up nearly half a block. This building is the other bookend and serves as a monument to *social stability*. If these are the two bookends, then what is the unspoken volume in between?

The Unspoken Volume of History: The Way that Nearly Turned Minneapolis Upside Down

What you don't see is that the police station squats on the very site of **The Way**—1913 Plymouth Avenue. **The Way** is the unspoken volume that cries out to be heard. If you don't know your history, you are not in tune with the voices of those who sought to transform community life on the Near North Side. Nor do you know how **The Way** represented the hopes and aspirations of many nearly forgotten people. Some continue to choose not to forget. This book seeks to be a testimony to them and the power of remembrance.

Part Two:
It Couldn't Happen Here

In The Beginning

[The following narrative of events that took place on Plymouth Avenue on August 2, 1966, was written by Syl Davis and printed in the first issue of the newspaper **The Way** *in August 1968.]*

"In the beginning there was no Way. And then there was..." How? Looking back into the past, imagine about two years ago—August 1966—on a very hot and humid evening of the North Side Picnic. Remember the annual gaiety of twinkling lights, carnival rides, and the suspenseful choosing of a King and Queen of the North Side? Those were merry days and the picnic was the merriest of all, in its glamorous setting of North Common Park.

However, all was not quite as festive as outwardly appeared. As daylight faded into the hot, quiet still of dusk, Plymouth Avenue was in its usual hush of activity—far removed from the dash and go of North Commons—with only a few passing cars and the sound of small children's voices that would occasionally break the silence.

A group of Black youths returning early from the park had taken up their usual positions of vigilance on the corner of Knox and Plymouth—standing, sitting, discussing the events of the day, the remembrances of the past, and hopes for tomorrow—a usual event that happens wherever brothers can congregate—spectators at a slowly fast-moving passing world.

Another group (8-10 years old) of children on the South Side of the street ran eagerly into the small neighborhood store, there to spend their wealth almost unnoticed by their older brothers. When out of the store they exploded—running, yelling, and the storekeeper right behind them with broom handle (or stick) in hand shouting in a language we all know.

Almost as suddenly, the older brothers were on their feet going over to find out what was the cause of this sudden explosion. They were stopping the younger kids asking them, '"What happened?" "What's wrong?" "What's the matter?"

Some of them moved over toward the storekeeper asking him what had happened as he stood just outside his store yelling at them. They demanded, "Hey, man, what's the matter with you? What do you think you're doing? You old—"

Shortly after this confrontation, a relative calm returned when more youths came up and began to talk with the first group. The police came; some stood guard at the store on Plymouth and Knox, others cruised up and down Plymouth. The young people, seeing this, began to tease the police that had come to guard the store. Some began to sit on the ground next to the squad car; others leaned against it. They began to take exception to the statements of one of the officers, and some began to rock the back of the squad car. The officer left—a brick was thrown, then another, and another; then a loud crash from the store across the street. And very suddenly Plymouth Avenue was alive.

Youth began running toward Penn Avenue, throwing bricks, rocks, and bottles at passing cars, at stores, and everything else that presented a target in their way. Police set up hurried road blocks on two ends of Plymouth, one at James and the other on Oliver—after which the youths began to settle down to rest and wait. For a long time, they waited, waited and nothing.

Finally, the police removed the blockades and withdrew from the area. (I later learned they had to rendezvous at the Standard Station at Fremont and Plymouth.)

Again bricks, rocks, and bottles began to fly towards the windows that remained and towards passing cars, etc. By this time the police had formed into squads to march down Plymouth; squad cars patrolled throughout the area, while the remaining foot-patrolmen marched on the sides and the rear of the formation, dropping off on each corner to clear the streets.

The next morning the acting chief of police, the governor of the state, and an alderman called a meeting of Black leaders and businessmen to discuss the violence of the night before, for it was at this time that Minneapolis found itself with its first real racial disturbance. It was not large by any means, but it was enough to stir the minds of the city fathers. I was invited because I was on the street the night before as a worker for Wells Memorial, a North Side social work agency. Some thirty to forty people were in attendance, ministers, social workers, legal organizations, businessmen, city officials, and others.

The question came why? How come? What do they want? No one could truly answer, for no one there really knew, not even me. There were no young people present at all. Many people tried to answer in very general terms, but admitted they didn't know. Three others and I left the mayor's office, and drove to the North Side. We saw two or three of the young people on the street and asked them to come to the mayor's office and speak up about their needs. After some assurances were made, they came. They spoke about the lack of facilities, parks, playgrounds, recreational equipment, jobs, etc. as part of the problem. They asked that a meeting be held in an area known as Oak Park on the North Side at 5:00 p.m. The governor agreed to an open meeting. The meeting was well attended by youth, young adults, old, Black, and White— many spoke and voiced their complaints about recreation, education, employment, welfare, street maintenance, and other areas. The youths requested that jobs be made available for unemployed people in the area and money be provided to establish a place for them to go for recreation, and scholarships made possible for youth wanting to attend school in the fall and that I become the director of the recreational facilities. It was promised that jobs would be made available within twenty-four hours. Scholarships were granted. There was no mention of the recreational facilities or the improvement of parks, playgrounds, etc.

That evening, however, a man who owned a building at Logan and Plymouth said we could use that until a better location was found. We had no equipment, and the place was small. We borrowed a record player and some pop was given, [and] so five hundred youth tried to dance inside without much success. The next day another meeting was called at the mayor's office. The mayor had returned to the city and had contacted some of the business, community and city agencies to help out in this critical time. Within twenty minutes sixty-four jobs were possible. By 6:00 p.m. that evening, three hundred jobs were available. The Youth Opportunity Center and the Minnesota State Employment Service were instructed to assist in the processing of these jobs. An office was set up at Wells Memorial. Later that day we were offered a building at 1913 Plymouth Avenue, that read "Fishing Unlimited," which was much larger and had some offices, for two months free.

The roof leaked [and] the windows were broken in spots, but better than before. We had no money, no office equipment, nothing; many people came to volunteer in those early days. Many of us stayed up during the time from August 2 until August 9—twenty-four hours, trying to help wherever we could. The Employment Office moved into our newly found home and set up shop. Some 235 persons were placed on jobs, most returned to school that fall, some continued, and are still employed today. Others were released because the jobs were only temporary, and a very few quit. Many things were going on at that time; people were requesting a variety of services that we couldn't possibly serve, but we tried. Some recreational equipment was given: ping-pong mostly, and dances were held every night, with four hundred to six hundred youths attending.

There was lots of fun in those early days, though they were very tiring. By day we tried to contact people in the community to organize. We attended meetings continuously all day and were up all night with the youth.

Yes, times were tough! As we moved on, we established an employment department, a community resources department, and recreation. The requests for help or assistance came in such volume, we had to stop and ask why? Many people said that the other places would not understand; we tried to work with other agencies to handle these problems; nothing happened. Remember we were not getting any money for this work at all. Yes, we know that this was to be only a short time thing to bring calm back to the city and appease the young people until school started. However, of the five people that were giving themselves to us and the youth, it was decided that we really should organize into a non-profit agency and try to help people help themselves.

We went to Mayor Naftalin and told him of our plan. He could not believe it. "This is a nightmare," he said. We asked for his support in helping to raise funds and equipment, building, etc. He finally agreed, at which point he contacted Ray Plank of Apache Corporation and asked for assistance. Between them and a few other wonderful people we were able to buy the building.

[The following statement, also written by Syl Davis, was set within the article.]

Of course, the disturbances were precipitated among the angry, young unemployed men of the neighborhood. The city reacted by taking the role of a conciliator; it never answered the backlog of grievances or made amends for its years of quiet and silent neglect. But conciliate, it did. Among the active promoters of a neighborhood youth center in the North Side were Mayor Arthur Naftalin and Ray Plank of the Apache Corporation. They were able to raise funds for a building and find temporary jobs for the unemployed young men. For the building, they chose to renovate a vacant business establishment (Fishing Unlimited) on Plymouth Avenue. The unusual name, **The Way**, was chosen by some of the young people of the neighborhood to symbolize a "Way out," but surely it means also a path—that is, traveling with a desired goal in mind. In retrospect, it was a happy choice, for the unexpected name defined the rich potentialities of the institution, but left many establishment, in-a-groove workers cold, for they could not find any rapport with its uncertain and unbureaucratic language.[1]

Part Three:
How The Way Got Its Name

The Way *is proud of its name*
because it was decided on by the young people
of the North Side community.
They believed that the center had to be more than a place,
it had to represent a "way of life" to the persons who came.
While those youths had only other youths like themselves in mind,
adults accepted the simplicity and directness of their choice
and began working toward seeking out other adults
to adhere to its meaning.

—Syl Davis[1]

What Do You Call This Place?

Mayor Arthur Naftalin, the first Jewish mayor of Minneapolis, and Ray Plank, a leading businessman, pooled their resources, involved others, and purchased a building on Plymouth Avenue. The building was near the outburst of street violence that erupted a few nights earlier. For the first time, young African-American men and women who were alienated from main stream society found a refuge.

I was there when **The Way** got its name. Several African-American young men were sweeping out 1913 Plymouth. The building still carried the previous tenant's sign, "Fishing Unlimited." The young men didn't see the mess; they saw only their own beautiful place.

Today nearly everyone owns their own phone. In the sixties, one didn't own their own phone. Telephones were owned by Ma Bell (telephone company) that would come to a new site and install their phones. A Ma Bell technician had come to 1913 Plymouth to install phones in various rooms, leaving them on the floor as there was yet no tables and chairs. Before leaving, the technician asked the young men what was the name of the place? He said he needed a name for the telephone listing. The young men looked at each other. It was the first time the idea had even been talked about. They began throwing names out when one of them said, "Let's call it **The Way.**" Nods of approval went about the circle. They knew it was the right name for the right place at the right time.

Part Four:
The Grand Jury Report On
The Way

Overstating the Case

An editorial in the *Minneapolis Tribune* echoed the words of novelist Elizabeth Hardwick had written following the riots in Watts, "it appears our dreams are never free of conspiracies."

> The grand jury report on the Minneapolis racial disturbances this summer shows once again that there are no easy explanations for Negro unrest here—no outside agitators, no conspiracies, no Communist elements.[1]

A month later another editorial appeared that struck a different note, a more skeptical surmise of the grand jury report on **The Way**.

> We believe that the Hennepin County Grand Jury was rather unfair to question the effectiveness of **the [Way]** center after such a limited time of operation. North Side settlement house workers say that **The Way** has yet to prove itself. This is true. But they add that it has the potential to reach people they have not reached, partly because it does not share the identification of their agencies with the outside "White establishment."[2]

The editorial sought to strike a balance with the Hennepin Grand Jury report on **The Way**. The *Tribune's* fairness doctrine makes the editorial sound lame against the accusatory prose of the grand jury report. The sole purpose of the report was to be a warning and a scold as it characterized **The Way** consorting with hoodlums, "those few trouble-makers who have caused and can cause this extensive damage."[3] The grand jury's agenda was not ambivalent. At the time, the dominant German-Scandinavian culture of Minnesota was rebounding from the shock waves of what the populace considered the senseless riots in North Minneapolis in the summers of 1966 and 1967. Part of the shock was the disbelief that it could happen here. The *Tribune* editorials seemed to labor under that same shock—not so the grand jury report. If the *Tribune* believed **The Way** had yet to prove itself, the grand jury was clear as to the nature of such proof—preventing further riots.

The *Tribune* editorials and the grand jury report reveal the race relations climate, to use the common parlance of the day, in Minneapolis during the middle sixties. The acumen of European societies, settled in Minnesota, contributed to the democratic tools of fair play and tolerance. However, beneath that veneer, what would later be called Minnesota "nice," went old exclusionary practices that segregated people by race and class. As a case in point, the dominant culture was so insular in Minneapolis that its own anti-Semitism was inadvertently revealed to itself when Arthur Naftlin, a Jew, was elected mayor in the early sixties. One of the perks that went with the office was the mayor was given an honorary membership in the Minneapolis Club, which, up to that time, had excluded Jews. The club could not very well exclude the mayor. That is how the Minneapolis Club quietly became integrated.[4]

The grand jury investigation of **The Way**, under the guidance of the county attorney, held biased views that were hardly disguised in the report—a bias alluded to in the Minnesota Civil Liberties position that was critical of the grand jury report on **The Way**.

> The grand jury perhaps unwittingly let itself become the vehicle for the expression of a point of view, which in the private sphere would be irreproachable but under the mantle of privilege immunity provided by law, inevitably takes on the shape and form of oppression.[5]

The grand jury's argument was straight forward. The violence of the riots of 1966 brought **The Way** into existence, a violence that was instigated by a certain criminal element. By implication, a mandate was given to keep such violent persons in check. Why else **The Way**? When the riots of 1967 erupted, what was a person who held such an implicit view to think? However, no evidence was found that **The Way** assisted in causing these riots on Plymouth Avenue in 1967. If the grand jury said no more, nothing else would have been said. But they could not keep still. They had to say something.

The Hennepin Grand Jury report revealed the thinking in certain sectors of the White power community that **The Way** was really behind the riots. By the grand jury's own implicit acknowledgment, it declared that **The Way** was a center of protest. First, the report offered a positive word. The report expressed belief that "the intended purpose of '**The Way**' was good." How can a simple sentence have so many different meanings to so many different people? Some on the grand jury may have believed **The Way** was a community center seeking to reach troubled young people. To others, the good **The Way** could do was keeping the bad characters in line, the criminals at bay, and, in this, they sided with the police who knew the troublemakers by name. A litany of police reports could tell of the confrontations and troubling understandings that kept a known bad character from going to jail or put another in jail. These reports also showed the protection given to one who had snitched so as not to go to jail. It revealed warfare on the streets between societies that still makes movies and sitcoms for those who are insulated from such violence.

The Way board of directors' critique of the grand jury report was sent to the Minnesota Civil Liberties Union. One of the key judgments of the board was the passing reference in the report that justified its stance and came in the phrase "there is fear." The report never articulated whether the fear was a general fear or a fear expressed by all or most of those who testified before the grand jury or whether it was a fear felt by the grand jury itself. The board went on record.

> We submit that the recommendation by a juridical body based on an unnamed generalized fear which brings into

question the work and reputation of a private agency tends to destroy the respect and sense of credibility that should be due a grand jury if our system of just law is to continue.[6]

Vindication came when the Minnesota Civil Liberties Union responded months later.

The Rebuttal:
The Minnesota Civil Liberties Union Response

Nowhere in the statues do we read that grand juries
are authorized to pass judgment or issue pronouncements
about persons or organizations
which are not accused of crimes.
Nevertheless this grand jury stated that one of its purposes
was "to determine whether [it] could make some
constructive suggestions."
We submit that the power of a grand jury
does not embrace advice to society,
and that however well intended,
a foray into the realms of social criticism is improper.

—Minnesota Civil Liberties Union[7]

The Way did not possess the necessary prestige in the public mind to have offered rebuttal in a convincing manner to a body that had legal status such as the grand jury. It needed an ally, someone beyond **The Way** staff and its board who could vouch for the justice of its case. The Minnesota Civil Liberties Union became such a voice. It rose to the occasion and without mincing words boldly criticized the grand jury and the county attorney for its grievous misuse of power. The statement of the Minnesota Civil Liberties Union needs to be quoted for its eloquence and sense of justice.

We Have Here a Misuse of Power

By its statements respecting **The Way**, the grand jury surrounded **The Way** with a cloud of suspicion which infringes seriously upon the civil liberties of that organization and of the people associated with it. Accusations or dark hints of wrong doing when uttered by an arm of the judiciary can only create apprehension in the public mind and must necessarily undermine public confidence and good will in an organization which is attempting to solve serious social problems with deep roots in civil liberties issues. Because **The Way** depends for its very existence on gifts and contributions from concerned citizens, anything which destroys public confidence inevitably cripples its effectiveness. Historically the most powerful weapon of tyranny has been economic deprivation, and this particular grand jury forged a most subtle instrument to deprive **The Way** of its economic base.

The Grand Jury Denied Due Process

The grand jury denied to **The Way** due process under the Fourteenth Amendment to the Constitution. By asserting that **The Way** had been criticized, and that allegations had been made about the relationship between criminal activity and **The Way**, the grand jury rendered it defenseless. **The Way** stands accused without trial. The American system of jurisprudence required that an accused be confronted by his accuser. Because the grand jury testimony has not been released, the charges against **The Way** are, in effect, secret. [Such testimony is still held in secret forty years later.] The Civil Liberties Union has repeatedly opposed the use of secret testimony to castigate people and organizations, and in its opposition to the House Un-American Activities Committee has stated this opinion in the strongest terms. It is regrettable that a grand jury employed tactics abhorrent to due process. The grand jury's assertion that "most of the Negro community wants it known that those persons connected with **The Way** do not speak for them" was no justification for the grand jury to play the role it did. The grand jury perhaps unwittingly let itself become the vehicle for the expression of a point view, which in the private sphere would be irreproachable but under the mantle of privileged immunity provided by law, inevitably takes on the shape and form of oppression. The fact that the grand jury "found no factual evidence" of wrongdoing should have enjoined it to be silent. Instead it chose to give a spurious credibility and substance to what can only be regarded as rumor and opinion, and this, we maintain, is injurious to due process.

The Grand Jury Transgressed The Equal Protection Doctrine

The grand jury compounded its error by urging the police "to keep a watchful eye" on **The Way**. This urging transgresses the equal protection doctrine, and it's tantamount to harassment. No citizen or organization can exercise civil liberties in any meaningful fashion under pressure of threatened interference by law enforcement agencies. In the absence of factual evidence of wrong doing, **The Way** and its staff are entitled to possess the same privileges and immunities enjoyed by the rest of the community. This they cannot do under the watchful eye of the police.

The Grand Jury Inflamed Fears That Restrict the Freedom to Innovate

The grand jury report is particularly obnoxious when it is considered in the ambience of the social climate into which it was injected. At a time in American life when problems beset us all, such a report can only inflame the fears that threaten the freedom to innovate and create new modes of approach to old problems. The evidence is by now overwhelming that minority groups in the United States have not enjoyed parity and equality in the area of civil liberties. Therefore it is all the more lamentable when a grand jury seeks out and strikes an organization in the community that is experimenting in new methodology to alleviate distress and social tensions.

The Grand Jury Commits Libel

The grand jury did, in effect, libel **The Way** and the people associated with it by deviously implying that the staff of **The Way** may be less than honest or of good character. To suggest that **The Way** ought to be discontinued or have its leadership changed if it continues "to show negative results in rehabilitating the hoodlum element" is both arrogant and unwarranted. It is not the duty of a grand jury to set goals and objectives for private organizations, or to recommend changes in its management on such superficial grounds. When all the rhetoric has been sifted out of the grand jury report we will find that **The Way** stands accused of nothing more than a degree of unpopularity. In such circumstances the government, or any arm of it, should be rather disposed to protect unpopular minority views instead of joining the hue and cry of the opposition. The use of innuendo by a grand jury to create suspicion and incite anxiety is improper. Freedom of expression cannot flourish in an atmosphere of official hostility.[8]

A Cautionary Tale

Strange as it may sound, in the struggle for freedom, often it is not the official word that has the final word. The public statement of the Minnesota Civil Liberties Union on **The Way** offers a cautionary tale that would warn those in high places who still seek to have the final word. The struggle for human liberties is a vital and global struggle and will always be so. For it can no longer be neglected, no longer be denied, without great cost to those who seek to defend freedom, for freedom is a struggle that insists on high costs. In a small corner of the globe more than a generation ago, **The Way** was engaged in that struggle for freedom.

The Way Comes to the Defense
of University of Minnesota Black Student Protesters

In April 1969, the Hennepin County Grand Jury indicted three Black University of Minnesota students involved in a takeover of Morrill Hall on campus. **The Way** board of directors went to the students' defense knowing firsthand how a grand jury can overstep its bounds and misuse its power. This is what the board wrote in protest.

Because a previous Hennepin County Grand Jury inappropriately and gratuitously attacked **The Way**, which has a predominantly Black constituency and which is an advocate of social change, we believe we can see an emerging pattern of misuse of the grand jury's great powers in the direction of suppressing minority group protests.

1. This board urges those is control of our judicial system to recognize that the White racism inherent in our institutions has, to a greater or lesser degree, become a "normal" part of all Whites (and of many minority persons); that racism, both overt and covert, too often motivates our actions; and that they must continually remind themselves and the jurors to "correct" for this built-in bias.

2. The county attorney be asked to utilize the Minneapolis Department of Civil Rights, the State Department of Human Rights, or any other such appropriate body to regularly background a jury as to the current, general interracial situations, to interpret for them the meaning of occurrences with racial overtones, and to explain the consequences of alternative grand jury decisions concerning them, especially if there is an appearance of anti-minority bias being involved.

3. That the entire judicial system be urged to bend over backward in ensuring that all proceedings meticulously conform to the spirit of the grand jury charge which states that the jury should be the protection of the innocent against persecution, and that it should see that its powers are in nowise perverted or abused because a grand jury might, unless motivated by the highest sense of justice,

find indictments not warranted by evidence and thus become a source of oppression to our citizens.[9]

Black Studies Come to U of M

After the black students took over Morrill Hall on the University of Minnesota campus, not knowing what to do next, they called **The Way**. Immediately, Mahmoud El-Kati went to talk and counsel the students. With his help they wrote a list of demands to be presented to Malcolm Moos, President of the University.

In spite of the grand jury indictments of the Black student protesters, the University of Minnesota, thanks to the foresight of its President Malcom Moos, turned the situation to good advantage. Many of the demands of the Black students were acted upon. In large measure, the present University of Minnesota's African-American Studies Department owes its existence to those students who were willing to pay the price that freedom demands.

Part Five:
The Way For Its Time

We can do what I can't.

—Syl Davis[1]

It was **The Way,** *under the stewardship of Syl Davis
which created for our entire community a unique bit of
Free Social Space.*
The Way *was the one place in the Twin Cities community
where people from all walks of life could gather, interact,
debate, and hold honest, if sometimes heated
and frustrated discussions.*
*It was the one place where disparate groups of people,
Black, White, and Red, Christians, Jews, and Muslims,
those living high and those living low, could need and look
at one another, instead of up or down.*
*Yes, the lowest, the least, and the lost,
and the rich people, who could still claim a human face,
held communion.*
*There absolutely was the measure of what this meant,
except to say, we know it meant something positive
and life giving.*
The ripples from waves of creative justice from **The Way**
and the spirit of Syl Davis are still being felt.

—Mahmoud El-Kati[2]

The Beginning of The Way

[Mahmoud El-Kati, the Education Director at **The Way** *1967-1970, wrote the following historical statement in 1984.]*

The origin of **The Way Opportunities Unlimited, Inc.** as a viable community social service organization is a classic example of societal challenge and response. The seeds of its beginnings are to be found in the turbulent climate and soil of social and political flux during the 1960s. In a time when principled and deeply felt questions on civil and human rights of Black Americans surfaced (once again), there were a myriad of actions and reactions, from every conceivable source in search of creative solutions to this historical problem. It can be said in earnest that **The Way** was in sum and substance, part and parcel of the spirit of awareness and the movement of ideas to address long standing inequities which flaws the ideals of democracy. In a word, the quest for social and/or racial justice. [sic] The origin and mission of **The Way** must therefore be viewed within the context of the National Civil Rights Movement. At its deepest level, the social movement for civil rights was a gallant effort to secure the already constitutionally guaranteed legal, civil, and social rights of an aggrieved class within the republic. In our community, **The Way** acted as a catalyst and creative agent for social change. To ignore the climate of that era, to forget its history, is to miss the origins, mission, meaning, and message of **The Way** as an agency, which responded to the challenge for social change.

The spirit of volunteerism, which is the balance wheel of reform in a free society, supplied the underlying energy, which gave birth to the very ideals that founded **The Way Opportunities Unlimited, Inc.** In August of 1966, an impressive cross-section of individuals, Black and White, rich and poor, prestigious and unsung, came together with common concerns to do something constructive and life-giving. They sought to make a sensitive and intelligent response to the demands of the times, more precisely, to make common cause in responding to the demands of their community. The collective efforts of these citizens, after much deliberation, focused their efforts on building an institution that would address the most conspicuously unmet needs of the most disorganized segment of the Near North Side Minneapolis community.

Those Who do not Have a Way

The focus is our youth. One of the most graphic revelations of the consequences of the making of proscribed communities called Urban Ghettos was the presence of a huge sub-stratum of alienated Black youths. Almost universally in this setting, the attendant themes in social problems prevailed: poverty, delinquency, unemployment, conflicts in criminal justice, inadequate education, low self-esteem, etc.

It was perceived by these humanly motivated movers and shakers, who organized **The Way**, that accompanying the more obvious aspects of social explosion during the mid-1960s, there was an implosion. The debilitating environment of Near North Minneapolis pressed inward on the community's most important resource, young people. Lack of opportunity for upward mobility, (especially if it is felt that these very limitations are imposed) breeds frustration, stifles imagination creating unfocused hostility.

Common sense and historical experience combine to suggest a simple but compelling view that the phenomenon of alienation in our society is the source of many of the anti-social tendencies engulfing the young. This can be even more uniquely and graphically the case in times of stress, as the 1960s occasioned. While it was true that a visible segment of the youth were engaged in creative and positive acts, within the context of a democratic movement (Civil Rights) for social change, many more were not. That is to say, the critical mass of our young people in large urban environments remained outside the pale of playing useful roles in everyday life. Many of our young were further disoriented by the explosive nature of the Civil Rights struggle. Often, misunderstanding the meaning of the large questions of freedom and social justice produced side effects among the uninitiated, which amounted to a crazy quilt manifestation of self-defeating impulses. This behavior further exacerbated conditions in an already fragile material and social environment.

The founders of **The Way**, daringly and correctly, defined for themselves the special mission of ameliorating the blinding chaos surrounding the young in community life. Problems in school, personal adjustment, poor social habits, and other more self-destructive acts, personally and socially, are related to environment. It was perceived that a change in environmental conditions also changes its environs. A focus on youth as social category meant a focus on conditions that shaped and molded their lives.

The approach of the beginners of **The Way** was thus based on the simple but profound philosophy of caring and sharing. It is a familiar ethic that is good and right to help others help themselves. This ethic, was of course, complimented by the obligation to share whatever could be offered that encourages human beings to reach their individual and collective potential. In principle and practice, an inclusionary spirit of assisting all who need or who sought help was the affect. This was to assure that the lowest, the least, and the lost would be served among others. Consequently, during the formative years of **The Way**, 1966-1970, concentrated efforts were made to reach and teach the unreachable. The neglected youth, more often than not, are those inclined toward wayward acts, in school, home, and the uncharted streets of urban life. This avenue became a priority, more out of necessity of the moment than by absolute design.

The social rumble of finding a place in the sun is ofttimes the most critical problem facing the young anywhere. This studied fact of life is compounded in communities such as Near North Minneapolis, where there are fewer alternatives for life chances.

The Way Begins Providing a Way

One of the first programs fostered by **The Way** was in the area of education. The establishment of remedial programs in basic education, special classes for the truant, all with the help of volunteers was the beginning step. Included in this effort was the incarcerated, isolated by circumstances, but no less deserving of attention. **The Way** was the first to offer non-traditional social service programs to the prison population, in local, state, and federal institutions of confinement.

This multi-dimensional concept of creative education as conceived by the forerunners was far reaching. At **The Way**, public classes were held for the community at large. In such classes, courses were offered, free of charge, to the immediate and surrounding communities, which drew in attendance many professional educators, social service workers, civil servants who run the government, and members from the business community. The subject matter was innovative, if not original, for its time. Course content long neglected by formal education was at the heart of the instruction—Afro-American, African, Native American, Hebrew, and Third World classes were offered. In addition, the general run of conventional courses, from sociology to criminology, was offered because of an obvious relevance to decoding social reality.

It can be said with certainty that **The Way** broke new curriculum grounds, preceding the adoption of the curriculum reform movement in the field of education during the late 1960s. This is attested to by the fact that the education department of **The Way** was invited to structure and teach courses in higher academic circles at a number of our state colleges and universities.

The Way Becomes a Known Way

There is a direct link between the efforts of **The Way** and the establishment of the African-American Studies Department at the University of Minnesota, which led to subsequent types of departments at the University, which parallels this department. The establishment of **Antioch-Minneapolis Communiversity** [a branch school of Antioch College in Yellow Springs, Ohio] was a by-product of **The Way's** pioneering thrust to steer education towards participatory democracy. This new thrust was achieved in addition to building the earliest curriculum revision committees in the Twin Cities public schools and working in an advisory capacity with many of the leaders of established educational systems, public and private.

The streams of **The Way's** energy during its formative stage of growth were both internally and externally directed. The inter-related climate of the times created this imperative.

While the primary and conscious aims were geared to improving the social health of immediate conditions surrounding life on the Near North Side, the questions inherent in this concern linked much of this energy and direction to the broader community.

The outreach efforts of **The Way** to work with individuals and groups, as well as institutions involved in seeking solutions to civil, social, and human rights questions, entailed in myriad of tactical approaches. Accordingly, **The Way,** by its actions, became a school of public instruction for people from many walks of life. Many of the community's major institutions, educational, governmental, civic, and businesses, were touched by activities emanating from **The Way**. One can cite the origin of several organizations or institutions still thriving, which the staff of **The Way** participated in founding or supporting during their embryonic stage. M.O.E.R. (Mobilization of Economic Opportunity), court services in Minneapolis, criminal justice system, the Minneapolis Urban Coalition, the North Side Resident Council, Pilot City Program, Legal Rights Center, are but several examples representing this style of collaboration. In surrounding suburbs, the educational staff of **The Way** held countless formal classes in Afro-American History and Sociology; workshops in human relations at churches schools, lodges, civil, and professional organizations.

Though generally understated, the achievements of **The Way** in these arenas helped to open new vistas of understanding in education and human relations. In retrospect, these deeds are perhaps **The Way's** greatest contribution to community awareness. Further, in social activism, **The Way** played a vanguard role in advocacy for the poor, the unrepresented, and unseen. **The Way** worked with and for the human reality behind the cold statistics. While the bulk of such accomplishments cannot be precisely or quantitatively measured, a qualitative impression can be gained from living voices from kindred spirits in sister community organizations and many individual community leaders in politics, welfare, education, criminal justice, business, and religion.

It has been said that all history is a current event. **The Way**, like many innovative and self-defining community organizations born across America during the sizzling 1960s still has a mission. It is a mission to promote the general welfare of its community. This mission embraces the board spectrum of public questions and social problems, which includes education, economics, community services, and advocacy in the area of welfare, criminal justice, youth development, and special services to the poor. This mission has been and still remains a wondrous adventure of the human spirit. The vicissitudes of becoming, not being, has been the essence of **The Way's** existence. It has not been easy. But on balance, the experience has meant a healthy admixture of challenges and rewards, obstacles and setback, undergirded by a tenacious will to succeed.

The domestic current event of this hour is indeed the history of **The Way.** Forms of social reality have changed. In its community, **The Way**, has played a crucial role in the process of this social change. Albeit, the substance of things remains the same. And so the struggle to reach fulfillment continues.

The Way is now closing in on its second decade as a creative social and cultural force in Twin City life. Thanks to many committed friends, supporters, and well-wishers, **The Way** has survived the hardships of growing pains. By wavering but steady steps, **The Way** has passed through the chaos of social unrest and through the innocent state of popular excitement with its underlying messianic message. It has, with limited financial support, passed through the state formalization. **The Way** articulates its program and operates from design.

Finally, **The Way** has reached the stage of institutionalization. It has established polices and lasting relationships with many traditional organizations, agencies, and community groups that are fully acquainted with its mission. In a very real sense, **The Way** is a part of the larger story that is deeply rooted in the American dream. It is optimistic, despite the world, about the possibilities for the future. As all persons who love humanity know, "humanity cannot advance without its dreamers," for if dreams die, humanity cannot exist. There is the earnest belief here, that given an opportunity, people are perfectly capable of discovering solutions to their own problems. We recall with even more profundity, and without apologies, that the ideals of the mission of **The Way** are inspired by echoes from the prophets of old.

"If I am not for myself,

who will be for me?

If I am for myself alone,

then what good am I?

If not now, when?

If not you, who?"[3]

A Time like No Other Time

Those early years of 1966 and 1967 was a time like no other time. **The Way's** notoriety had come upon us like a sudden storm that took us by surprise. The staff and some of its board members became quite adept at telling the story of **The Way**. Gwyn Jones-Davis took Spike Moss under her wing to teach him how to speak to various audiences. She developed a speaker's bureau. Soon Spike and Gwyn, along with Syl Davis and other staff persons, traveled to numerous groups in the Twin Cities and throughout the state.

The Way attracted a great deal of public notice that perked the interest of numerous groups that came to see what **The Way** was about. On one occasion, Gwyn, Syl, and I suddenly found ourselves in front of a group of Christian newspaper editors from around the United States. The editors were in the Twin Cities at a conference hosted by the Billy Graham Association and heard about **The Way** from their host. The entire group of fifty or so newspaper editors decided to come right over. I remember telling them that the early Christian movement was called "followers of the Way." **The Way** was a movement of liberation that had its roots in that first movement that started to change the world two thousand years ago.

Attention and publicity can charm and so offer the illusion of self-importance. Those heady early days seemed as if the world's axis moved about a small vortex of power on Plymouth Avenue in Near North Minneapolis. For that one moment **The Way** was the way for its time.

The Way was Not To Be the Way

*All history knows that humanity cannot advance
without its dreamers, for if dreams die, humanity dies.*

—Mahmoud El-Kati[4]

The final chapter of **The Way** was written in 1989 when a reconstituted board of directors, largely made up of persons from the Near

North Side of Minneapolis, under the leadership of Verlena Matey-Keke made an organized effort to reopen **The Way** building. The building had been closed since 1984.

Syl Davis, who had served as president of board since 1982, left the board in May 1984 over a disagreement he had with Director Harry "Spike" Moss before the new building had been constructed. Ominously, the dedication of the new building never took place. In December 1984, the United Way cut off its funds to **The Way** claiming mismanagement of United Way monies. The cut off of program funds kept the building from opening. **The Way** became history.

Five years later the reconstituted board of directors sought to have the building reopened and given back to **The Way's** board through the help of the Minnesota Attorney General's Office. It was at this time a youth organization known as The City brought a proposal to merge with **The Way.** The merger would create a new organization thus giving legitimacy to reopening **The Way** building under a new name. The City began as a youth drop-in center under the leadership of Father Joseph Selvaggio on the South Side of Minneapolis in the middle sixties. By 1989, it was a full-fledged United Way agency with a primary focus in offering alternative learning strategies for youth of all races in conjunction with the Minneapolis Public Schools. The reconstituted board of **The Way** rejected the proposal.

The issue went to court. During the court hearing Russ Ewald, director of the McKnight Foundation, who had years earlier negotiated **The New Way** in becoming a United Way agency, approached Syl Davis to say that the building could be **The Way** board's if they would only give up the name **The Way.** This remark stunned Syl. Syl said, "**The Way** belonged to the people on the Near North Side who named it. **The Way** is theirs, and no one else could change its name."[5] To change the name of **The Way** would be a final giving over to the establishment that Syl had warned was beginning to happen to **The Way** as early as 1970. The court turned down the reconstituted board's request to reopen **The Way**. Instead, the court awarded the building to the Harry Davis Foundation.

It was clear that the court could not award what was a Black organization to what was clearly perceived as a White organization unless there would be a Black intermediary. That would be the Harry Davis Foundation. Harry Davis had made his views known when **The Way** closed at the end of 1984.

> Harry Davis, a Black executive for Cowles Media Co. who works with the United Way and other city organizations, said **The Way** should continue to serve the North Side but must change if it hopes to do so. "Look at other organizations on the North Side," Davis was quoted to say, "they have changed tremendously. Now they have professional counselors, professional social workers; they de-emphasize a lot of physical activities." [The last statement is a surprise coming from a man who for years dedicated himself to teaching young Black males how to box at Phyllis Wheatley, a North Side Community Center.] Harry Davis was further quoted, "I don't think **The Way** has become more professional. The other agencies followed the plans and priorities of the United Way whereas **The Way** had a variance."[6]

The Way building would be given to a more professional organization. This is exactly what the Harry Davis Foundation did. It turned **The Way** facility over to The City that continues as of this writing to operate in the building **The Way** had built but was never given the opportunity to use.

The Way is no longer here to advocate its vision. The void it leaves behind is yet another certainty that only exacerbates conditions that still need to be addressed. Gone is **The Way**, and gone are the innovative and self-defining work it did at its best moments in co-partnership with the community. Gone is the mission to promote the general welfare of the Near North Side community. Gone is the engagement of public questions and social problems. Gone is the advocacy for those caught in the criminal justice maze or lost beneath the piles of welfare forms and standards that have little understanding and compassion for the poor. Gone is the quixotic spirit to charge the windmills of institutional inertia that is incredibly out of date with the needed human reform for equality and justice.

The nearly forgotten history of **The Way** is a witness to the dreams and hopes of oppressed people. It is their story, and so it must not be forgotten.

FOUR

THE WAY OF STRUGGLE

*It is more a figure of speech to say
that Negroes are as a people chained together.
We are one people—
one in general complexion, one in common degradation,
one in popular estimation.
As one rises, all must rise,
and as one falls all must fall. . . .
Every one of us should be ashamed to consider himself free,
while his brother is a slave.
The wrongs of our brethren, should be our constant theme.
There should be no time too precious,
no calling too holy, no place too sacred,
to make room for the cause.*

—Fredrick Douglas[1]

The Way and Ishmael The Street Brother

The present day manchild is a human paradox. . .
he is considerably more sophisticated adolescent.
He has more knowledge, more sensitivity,
he is more amicable, more likely to commit murder. . .

—Minneapolis Star Tribune[1]

The Way Comes Under Fire
For Reaching Out to the Unreachable

In 1967, **The Way's** very existence was troubling to many in and out of power. The fact that people of influence had vigorously advocated for **The Way** did not stop others in finding ways to discredit it. The Hennepin County Grand Jury was called to investigate the causes for the riots on Plymouth Avenue in 1967. The grand jury brought no criminal charges, yet it publicly accused **The Way** of harboring, if not nurturing, criminals. The county attorney brought in persons to testify that "most of the Negro community wants it known that *those persons* [italics mine] connected with **The Way** do not speak for them."[2] It was an obvious maneuver to divide and conquer and so discredit **The Way**. Amazing how the truth has a way of getting heard at the oddest moments. The flaccid charge was countered by the simple declaration that **The Way** did not seek to speak for the Negro community. What was lost on the grand jury was that **The Way** identified itself with Black Power, not with the Negro community. Those who chose to be called "Negro" represented a middle class orientation, that in their hostility toward **The Way**, had found it was playing a collaborative role with the powers downtown. Concurring with the grand jury, some Negro leaders publicly accused **The Way** of coddling criminals. Just who were these criminals?

About the time the grand jury was meeting behind closed doors, Syl Davis was interviewed by Gerald Vizenor for the magazine the *Twin Citian*. Gerald Vizenor, himself a Native American, is now a published author and professor at the University of California, Berkley campus. Mr. Vizenor asked Syl a direct question, "Do you think this society still needs a nigger?" Syl's answer was unflinching and straight forward. "I think they have to have a nigger to look at but they're damned well worried about it right now. ... It's like saying that a White man in America has to be better than someone else. ... The Black man just doesn't want to be a social nigger and folksy talk about pulling yourself up with your bootstraps."[3] Syl Davis didn't see criminals **The Way** was accused of coddling. He saw young Black men trying to find themselves and their way in an inhospitable world.

Ishmael: The Manchild Born to a Bondswoman

Frantz Fanon was a psychiatrist. He knew two worlds. One European—France where he studied medicine specializing in psychiatry; the other—his home Martinique. He made use of both experiences by interfacing them in his writing. His use of dialectical exchange between both worlds is evidenced in the title of his book *Black Skins, White Masks*. In the book he offers a telling contrast between Adlerian psychology with the psychology known by Black people of the Antilles. The Adlerian model is exclusively personal as it did not include the social context and its influence on the individual. On the other hand, the Antillean comparison, true also for Black people in the United States, is not personal but social. The governing fiction that determines identities in that world is slavery and is perpetuated today under the guise of racism. Fanon demonstrates the difference. The Adlerian comparison can be schematized in this fashion: "Ego greater than The Other." However, the Antillean comparsion, in contrast, would look like this: White is the ruling term thus changing the equation to "Ego different from The Other."[4]

Fanon uses dialectics the philosopher Hegel used in exploring master-slave relationships, but with a telling difference. "I hope I have shown that here the master differs basically from the master described by Hegel. For Hegel there is reciprocity; here the master laughs at the consciousness of the slave. What he wants from the slave is not recognition but work."[5] Within the Hegelian context, persons seek to impose their existence on another, to be recognized by another. It is the other who holds power in conferring or withholding recognition. You put slavery in that equation, as Fanon does, and those who were former masters act as if they still confer or withhold recognition, just as former slaves seek to make oneself recognizable.

There is a recognition scene in Ralph Ellison's novel *Invisible Man* when his main character, a Black man, accidentally bumps into a White man who then calls the main character an insulting name. The main character grabs the man by his coat and yells at him, "Apologize! Apologize!" But the White man only curses him, so the main character knocks the White man down and begins kicking him because the White man would not stop cursing him. The main character draws a knife but holds back when he realizes the White man has not really seen him. After beating the White man within an inch of his life, the main character left him, walking away wondering if the White man would awake to his life just before death. This is how Ellison describes what happens next. "The next day I saw his picture in the *Daily News*, beneath a caption stating that he had been 'mugged.' Poor fool, poor blind fool, I thought with sincere compassion, mugged by an invisible man!"[6]

The governing fiction needed a figure to confer on this invisible man. What better place to find a figure for an invisible man than in the Bible that often conversed with the invisible. In Genesis, the first book of the Bible, Abraham was promised by God to have descendents as numerous as the stars. Sarah, his wife, was unable to have children. In the sixteenth and seventeenth chapters of Genesis we read how Sarah encourages Abraham to have a child by his slave woman, Hagar. Hagar becomes pregnant and proud before Abraham's number one wife. Sarah and Hagar don't get on, their relationship becomes glances, unspoken asides of pride, and jealousy. Sarah has enough and deals harshly with Hagar, who flees. In the wilderness, an angel comes to Hagar to tell her to return and submit to Sarah. If she does, a promise will be hers. Hagar shall have descendents that will multiply beyond number. The angel gives a name to her child, Ishmael. Later, Sarah is blessed in her old age with a son named Isaac who will be the inheritor of the covenant first given by God to Abraham. But what of Abraham's first born? God promises to Hagar, Ishmael's mother, that her son will be the father of a great nation.

The consequences of this story leave their marks on history. One only has to check out how the three major Western religious traditions handle this story to their own advantage. Jews believe they are descended from Isaac, who was the son of promise born of Abraham's free woman, Sarah. However, following the prophet Mohammed, Islam believed itself to be the great nation of promise through Ishmael. Whereas, the Apostle Paul, trained as a Pharisee, was quick at the reversal of the story's definition. Turning everything upside down, Paul makes it known that Jews were no longer free but had become slaves to the law, while Christians being born of the Spirit were made free in Christ.

> For it is written that Abraham had two sons, one by a slave and one by a free woman. But the son of the slave was born according to the flesh, the son of the free woman through promise. Now this is an allegory: these women are two covenants. One is from Mount Sinai, bearing children for slavery; she is Hagar. Now Hagar is Mount Sinai in Arabia; she corresponds to the present Jerusalem, for she is in slavery with her children. But the Jerusalem above is free, and she is our mother.[7]

Scriptural polemics can be devastating but in the hands of a slave owner in the American South, it turned most cruel. Ishmael now becomes in the New World the illegitimate son born to a slave woman whom the master will not recognize as his own. Slavery is now gone, but the stigmata of its scar remains. The street brother seeks to be recognized, but he is only seen when he acts the part of his forebearer, Ishmael, the eternal outcast and rebel. "He [Ishmael] shall be a wild ass of a man, his hand against every man, and every man's hand against him; and he shall dwell over against all his kinsman."[8]

The Making of an American Ishmael

It was 1963 and I came across a fetching excerpt from James Baldwin's book *Fire Next Time* in the *New Yorker*. The book was an extraordinary telling of his early days growing up on the streets of Harlem, sketched in words that jived and danced powerfully across the magazine page. I read the words of this Ishmael from Harlem and began to understand, an understanding that proved vital as I worked with other Ishmaels on the Near North Side.

Baldwin's words describe the making of the contemporary Ishmael. It was the summer he came of age. He sensed the danger of the Avenue, as he called it, with its pimps and its whores. It was the summer that crime became real, not simply a possibility but as the only possibility. Two summers before, the ten-year-old Baldwin had been frisked by two White policemen who made comic and terrifying comments about his ancestry before leaving him flat on his back in an empty lot. It was the summer he decided he would go to hell before he would let the White man tell him who he was, forcing him to disappear into the ghetto. It was the summer he decided to be a man on his own terms.

An Ishmael Who Didn't Make It

In 1971, Johnny Lee Breedlove was killed by contract to still his mouth because he knew too much about the local drug underworld—the addicts and pushers along with their accomplices, the compromises, and bad deals. Johnny was a flawed man with a wife and a new baby. The Breedloves had just begun a new life together when Johnny was murdered. One Sunday after his death, his wife, Susan, stood up during a worship service in the Peoples Church to make a plea. "What will the church do? I do not mean finding Johnny's killer. I will never know who that was. But what will the church do so there won't be anymore Johns and Janes getting hooked on drugs in this community?" Within nine months the church created, with the help of several street brothers, a drug treatment program called the Half Way Inn. Johnny's death would give others a second chance at life.

Ishmaels I Came to Know: The Half Way Inn

James Spaulding, Wade Russell, Felix James, Eddie King, Mousey Patterson, Michael Crawford were all Ishmaels—street brothers I first met at **The Way**. They already were hardened by life on the streets, their rhetoric of bravado and charm a defense, grown callous toward those they considered their enemy, wary under the continual surveillance by the police who knew each of them by their first name. Our paths would crisscross over the years until 1971, when several of us worked together at the Peoples Church in a drug program called the Half Way Inn.

As the minister of the church, it fell on me to be the project director seeking to be an interpreter of the system to the brothers who served as counselors and who, in large measure, ran the program. On the other side, I sought to provide some light on the actions of the brothers to a system, described by James Spaulding, "as the band plays on, the system can't dance." Those words were written from the Minneapolis workhouse in response to the cutting of funds that spelled the end to the Half Way Inn after four brief months of operation; the program not even half-way started.

Just after the Half Way Inn was funded the brothers went downtown to the administrative office of Hennepin County to demand they be paid weekly, rather than bimonthly. Ishmaels don't write memos and sit behind desks. They bring their concerns directly to the parties they are dealing with. Their reasoning was straightforward. It was their money awarded by the state crime commission and they could do with it as they pleased. They seldom earned regular paychecks and had never mastered living inside a budget. They were not asking for more money, but simply to be paid more frequently. Hennepin County personnel were not prepared for this, and the bureaucrats became convinced on that day that this program was a high risk venture that needed to be watched.

Then a week later one of the Half Way Inn brothers hired a limousine and chauffeur to travel to Stillwater Prison. The brother wanted to take a person on the program and his family to see another family member who was in prison. Being on the staff of the Half Way Inn, the brother had something he never had before—credit. Surprising as it may sound, street brothers who have no credit can hire a limousine far easier than renting a car. Limousine services operate on a cash basis, and they do their own driving. In this case, the limousine company was more than willing to send the bill to the crime commission in St. Paul. The brother knew no different. The crime commission was not prepared to receive bills. That wasn't how the game was played. The staff of the commission simply disbursed money through another governmental agency, it didn't pay bills. Obviously, this program was not playing by the rules. Can you imagine all those claws in the ceiling, like frightened cats, of bureaucrats who on more normal days worked behind their desks?

Once the Half Way Inn brothers found out limousines were not acceptable, they asked what other alternative they had since the program had need of vehicles. They were informed vehicles could be secured from the equipment division of the county. The Half Way Inn brothers did just that. However, one vehicle was not returned but was simply left on the street with a dead battery. Was someone not thinking? Probably. I can only surmise what was happening. The fact that the Half Way Inn brothers certainly exercised bad judgment, and did so not fully understanding the consequences of what would soon overtake the program, is apparent. Ishmaels look out for themselves and are not totally aware how others are affected by their behavior. No doubt, soon after these incidents, secret meetings began taking place behind closed doors about what to do with those "bad boys."

It got worse when two Half Way Inn brothers were given monies to travel to a drug conference in San Francisco. The problem came about when they never got there. It seems they went to Los Angeles instead. Why? They probably knew friends there they wanted to see. One could say, though I won't, they planned on getting to San Francisco. One brother called to say his airplane ticket had been stolen. He was given another $200 so he could get home. When he returned, he said he had found his plane ticket. However, he never returned the $200. Not thinking? He was thinking all right—for himself. An Ishmael's life is one forever seeking cover, filtered by rationalizations and lies, so wary of what is going on at the moment, they seldom see what is coming.

There is another side to this story. A devastating reality made a visit as soon as it was public knowledge in December 1971 that the Half Way Inn was publicly funded. Over the next two weeks everyone associated with the Half Way Inn was arrested. The arrests took place within a block from the church. The police knew everyone by name, save some of the White persons who were in treatment and who did not live in the community. The arrests were a warning served by the police that the Half Way Inn was not wanted and that they were keeping an eye on everyone associated with it. Ishmaels are forever finding themselves behind the eight ball.

What signaled the end of government support for the Half Way Inn came on Good Friday of 1972. I was in my study at the church preparing for Easter services when I received a call. The call came from a woman who said the "so-called brothers" of the Half Way Inn had in their company the daughter of her friends from Des Moines, Iowa. As I learned later, the young woman, a minor who was fifteen or sixteen years old, had gone to a dance and there met some of the Half Way Inn brothers. She wandered off with them and had not come home. The police were already looking for her. The woman's voice grew firm, informing me in no uncertain terms that she and the parents were coming directly to the church and their daughter had best be there or the police would be called. I said I, too, was concerned for her daughter and would do everything I could to get in touch with the brothers in question. I called. One of the Half Way Inn brothers answered. I told him a young woman was last seen in their company and that her parents and a friend were coming to the church to pick her up. A blustery answer came back over the phone full of denials of knowing anything about the young woman. I said, "If she doesn't show, the police would be here." I left it at that.

The family showed up within a half-hour and moments later James Spaudling and Eddie King came marching into the study. Spaulding looked like a Mexican revolutionary wearing two belts of bullets crisscrossing his chest and two holstered guns at his side. Behind him quickly followed the young woman in question. Words were exchanged and the father pulled a small pistol as Eddie King grabbed him. They wrestled about as Spaulding, standing defiantly at the door of the small study, took out his two guns and began firing in the air. I later learned the guns Spaulding was firing had blanks, but not so the pistol of the father from Des Moines was firing. In the scuffle the father's gun went off three times in a space of seconds. One of his bullets lodged in the top of the door frame where I stood holding Spaulding's face in my hand shouting, "Why? Why?" Why I was holding his face with bullets flying overhead is something I cannot explain to this day.

No one was hurt. That's the miracle. The parents and their friend got out with the daughter in tow from under the bluster of the brothers. After the family and friend drove away the brothers simply walked off feeling indignant in being shot at rather than giving a reason why the young woman was with them. Alone, I could only think what was good about this Good Friday, save no one was shot.

The woman who called and who accompanied the parents from Des Moines to retrieve their daughter worked for the state—you guessed it—at the state crime commission. Within the week the commission had cut off all funds to the Half Way Inn.

James Spaulding had an intelligence and gift to make something of his life, but he never left the streets long enough to develop those gifts, never left the violence behind. Like so many Black men, he had been in prison as a young man and learned how to survive the hard side of life. He had been hurt, and he hurt others. He had been intent, for it went with the territory, always to be on the winning side of personal fights. He had learned, as Baldwin said, he needed an advantage, "a lever, something to inspire fear." But the one experience he never had, possibly never imagined he would, was being on the winning side in a social fight; save once.

It was in October 1971 when we went to the Hennepin County commissioners to secure their approval to be the fiscal agent for the Half Way Inn. The state crime commission had given the program monies, but it required a governmental agent to administer the funds. At that time the mayor of Minneapolis was a member of the police federation. There was no way for a program run by street brothers, who had continual run-ins with the law, would ever be approved by the city. So we went to the county commissioners.

Edward Gearty was the chair of the board of the Half Way Inn. He had practiced law on the Minneapolis North Side for over a quarter of century. Gearty never backed away from a fight if he thought the fight was for the right. As a young man, Edward Gearty saw action in the Minneapolis street battles during the Trucker's Strike in the early thirties. He traded fisticuffs for the battle of the courtroom. As a lifelong Democrat, he later served as the presiding officer of the House of Representatives in the Minnesota State Legislature. Gearty was a professional politician, and he knew all the commissioners by name. He wanted to know where the commissioners stood. As the commissioners voted to approve tens of thousands of dollars for the new government center, Gearty went to talk to each of them. He came to tell me there were two commissioners in our corner, two definitely opposed, and one on the fence who thought the program was too risky. Gearty said it would take a miracle for the commissioners to vote in our favor.

When the Half Way Inn proposal was on the table, one of the commissioners, once he started, couldn't stop bad mouthing the program because of the kind of people who were running it. Sitting next to me was James Spaulding who had a quick and hot temper. I thought, what would happen if he answered back? Suddenly, Spaulding stood up and I thought—*it's over*. But he didn't say anything. He simply walked out. Spaulding had decided he wasn't going to be party to such abuse. As he was walking out, the commissioner became livid, irrational, saying that such behavior was exactly what he was talking about. A vote was taken. The motion passed. The undecided commissioner had decided to vote for the Half Way Inn proposal. The diatribe of his colleague was so embarrassing he could not publicly associate himself with it.

I can still see Spaulding's face when we told him what happened. He was sitting outside on the courthouse steps. We told him the commissioners had just agreed to have the county be the fiscal agent and the program would start January 1. He looked at us in disbelief, his eyes searching for something he did not fully understand. Spaulding was always quick with words with a ready wit, his retorts sharp and barbed, never one for a loss of words. It was one of the few times I saw him let his guard down. I believe for the first time in his life James Spaulding found himself on the winning side in a fight for justice. He became part of a fight that was won with something more than muscles or intimidation. For once in his life James Spaulding had nothing to say.

The good news was short-lived. It would only be a few months before Spaulding would be writing his own letter of protest from jail. James Spaulding had his own principles, but, when coupled with the outrage of his ego, he would strike back. He felt only outrage when the Half Way Inn was shut down with no regard for its principles.

Your paper [Minneapolis *Star*] played on the seeming ambiguity of our title "The Brotherhood," since an old movie named *The Brotherhood* and a newer movie entitled *The God-father* (now playing in the Twin Cities) are based on the same subject; i.e. criminal subculture, the inference is obvious that the Half Way Inn's Brotherhood is a bunch of Black militant thugs! Why not call us Proto-Mafia Niggers, and be done with it? This is especially objectionable because your article states that Half Way Inn's programs, "includes, they say, many White youthful suburban patients," thus inferring that this was a fabrication on our part, to conceal the real nature of our organization. In point of faith, three-fifths of our methadone clients are "White suburban youth" and thus constitute a clear majority of our Black militant organization.

The Half Way Inn has enjoyed an unequaled rate of success in dealing with the narcotic problems in the community, and has done so for a year prior to asking for, or receiving, a penny in governmental backing. It is unfortunate that you ignore this fact, and the fact that were this not the case, the government would not have given any support to our program, which had turned to be the last chance and source of aid to the racial majority on the program. Some of these addicts had been ostracized by their own people and came to the militant Half Way Inn as the only source of aid left open to them, the only ones willing to help them with their problem, our Black militancy notwithstanding. Accepting White addicts into our program demonstrates, I hope, to all the true meaning of our title, "The Brotherhood." The Half Way Inn has been regurgitated from the stomach of the system and spewed back into the streets. So the band plays on and the system still can't DANCE!!"[9]

Thirty-Five Years Later:
The African-American Men's Project

The African-American Men's Project [2001] is a program conducted under the auspices of Hennepin County. It is yet another belated response to a growing crisis that, in its progress report, is more descriptive than prescriptive. It falls on the heels of the Human Rights Watch report [2000] that offers the startling fact that in the state of Minnesota a young Black male's odds of being locked up in prison is 27 to 1 against a young White male who has been arrested on the same charge.

Minnesota has the worst record of racial disparity of the fifty states studied. Only the District of Columbia has a record that is worse.

The fact that the African-American Men's Project was initiated the very year the author of *Manchild in the Promised Land,* Claude Brown, died carries a certain painful irony. Brown offered a revealing portrait of the Ishmaels that haunt the landscape of urban America, finding the only places that will take them in is the military or prison. The phenomenon of alienation, Brown understood and articulated, is the outward manifestation of an inward rage that quickly understands there is little room and far fewer useful roles in a society for Black men. Four decades ago **The Way** sought to creatively address the violence that permanently scars Black men. It is unfortunate the African-American Men's Project suffers from what one could call historical amnesia for making no mention of **The Way's** work with young Black people nor giving any credit to its pioneering efforts, let alone benefit from its work.

The Way's work goes on in the lives of people today; though the work is now scattered in shards of its former self, hardly reflecting the whole that once was the creative and powerful endeavor of justice for oppressed people. A lesser light, certainly, yet a light shines in the better moments of three proteges of **The Way**. Shane Price carries on the work as one of the leaders of the African-American Men's Project as does Peter Hayden, the director of Turning Point, a treatment center for recovering addicts. Spike Moss continues to weather decades of controversy offering leadership in times of crisis, though no longer a paid staff member of The City, a group that now operates out of **The Way's** former building. Some Ishmaels have survived, a few have even thrived, yet there are still too many who died violently and much too young.

The Way and The Law

Law is born from despair of human nature.

—Ortega y Gasset[1]

The Script has Not Changed:
Fifteen Minutes of Negative Fame

Déjà vu. August, 2002. The *Minneapolis Star Tribune* editorial labels the near-riot in the Jordan neighborhood as "Fifteen Minutes of Negative Fame."[2] The script and the cast are the same, only the names are changed. The stage is set. Summer time and the living is uneasy on the Near North Side of Minneapolis. A shooting of a Black youth in the community by the police pours fuel on the combustible conditions. The *Star Tribune* reports a person from the community states they overheard a police officer saying something about getting even. Just a week before a Black woman shot and killed a White woman officer who was placing the Black woman under arrest in South Minneapolis. The officer shot and killed the Black woman just before the officer died.

Act I Confrontation. The spark that ignites the blaze is a police raid on a crack house. Several police cars converge suddenly. The police rush the house with guns drawn. A resident sitting on the porch unleashes his pit bull that runs at the police as they come into the yard. The police shoot the dog, but one bullet ricochets and hits an eleven-year-old boy who is standing nearby. A police officer takes care to see the child is all right as other officers raid the house. TV crews and reporters arrive to cover the scene. The community is stirred by an ill wind of a child being shot by the police. A crowd gathers and shouts angry words and obscenities at the police and reporters. Someone throws a bottle at the police. Then another bottle is thrown. Suddenly, the angry crowd is throwing whatever it can get its hands on at the police who withdraw so things can cool off. The crowd turns on TV reporters who are filming the scene. A TV reporter is hit on the head. Another is beaten. They are both taken to nearby hospitals for treatment. A TV news van, its logo prominently displayed, is surrounded and a window shattered before the TV journalists can get away.

Act II Cool Down. Police officers who raided the house are put on a routine three-day paid leave. Minneapolis police begin their own investigation. The mayor talks of a federal mediator coming to Minneapolis. Veteran Black leaders Spike Moss and Shane Price come forward to lead citizen patrols that are organized to maintain some sense of calm over the weekend. Community leaders become resentful of those persons who do not live in the neighborhood but are recruited to be on the citizen patrols. Community leaders make it known that so-called Black leaders have come into their neighborhood at a moment of crisis, only to move on once the media leaves.

Act III Attaching Blame. Media blitz begins. Coverage includes the history of the crack house. A story appears in the Minneapolis newspaper about a reporter who had been beaten ten years before by one of the members of the house that had been raided. That household member, coincidentally, had just come back home. He had been living and working out state following his release from prison after serving out his sentence for the beating of the reporter. A feature article on Spike Moss and his familiar role in times of crises offers more questions than answers. The police federation becomes upset with the chief of police for giving out ID cards to the citizen patrols. The federation expresses resentment that police need help to do their job. The local chapter of the NAACP calls for an investigation seeking an independent organization to look at police practices. Long time residents say they are going to move. The newspaper is quick to report a resident's, who is packing up to move to Georgia after living in the neighborhood for seven years, sentiments. "This little infestation didn't just start last week; it's been horrible and getting worse for years. We're in an impoverished, low-income area—quote, unquote the hood—but that doesn't mean everybody is the same. A lot of people are here by force, not by choice." Another neighborhood voice, Don Samuels, wrote a letter to the editor.[3] He claims being the descendent of a mulatto house slave and the son of a White slave driver. His great grandfather was given a plot of land that launched the family into the free world. He knew his world changed for the better by the hard work of his forebearers. He said he understood not everyone is the inheritor of a past free of indebtedness and oppression. Mr. Samuels later is elected to the Minneapolis city council representing the ward that includes the Jordan community.

It All Happened Before

This scene played itself out countless times over the years. Following the assassination of Dr. Martin Luther King, Jr., **The Way** responded to similar racial tensions in the creation of the Soul Patrol. Its forerunner was the Black Patrol, organized the previous summer of 1967 by Dan Pothier, a staff member of **The Way**. He had good reason as he was shot at on Plymouth Avenue, reportedly by a White man driving by. One of the bullets narrowly missed Dan, hitting his steering wheel. There were other shooting incidents. A rumor spread through the community that gangs of White teenagers were roaming throughout the community. A Black teenager, while standing at **The Way's** entrance, was severely hurt in the face from flying debris, the result of a gunshot. Clearly something needed to be done to deter further violence perpetrated by persons outside the community.

Dan Pothier mobilized young Black men of the Near North Side and had them patrol the neighborhood in cars. It was the beginning of the Black Patrol. Police permits or ID cards were as controversial forty years ago as they are today. In 1967, the Black Patrol was given letters of identification that were later revoked. A conflict between the Minneapolis police inspector and the Black Patrol may have had something to do with it. It all started when three off-duty policemen from Golden Valley openly propositioned a Black woman on Plymouth Avenue. The Black Patrol was on duty and saw it happen. The Black Patrol took the men aside and, finding out they were police, started to threaten them with exposure. Things got heated, and the police were hit a few times by members of the patrol. Dan Pothier rushed to the scene after receiving a call from a member of the patrol. He was steaming mad himself and had to cool off before he got there so he could chill tempers down. "What do you want to do? Off these dudes? Then we're acting like them. Everything we gained you can lose right here. Think about it." He spoke nonstop to the men of the Black Patrol who held the policemen. In the meantime, someone called the Minneapolis police inspector. Inspector Dwyer showed up a short time later and, seeing the three police officers being held under arrest became livid. He took the policemen into custody and they were suspended for a short period of time. No one on the Black Patrol was charged with hitting the policemen. Years later, Dan Pothier reflected on what could have come down that summer night in 1967. "Everything we had gained could have been blown away that night. It was that close. Angers and hatred were boiling over."[4] Cooler heads prevailed that night. The outcome was a trade-off. The Black Patrol lost their letters of identification, and the Golden Valley policemen never returned to Plymouth Avenue.

Later that summer the Black Patrol became incorporated into what was called the Citizen's Patrol Corps that operated on both the north and south sides of Minneapolis. The patrols were linked by radio using a citizen band. The Soul Force would use similar means of communication the next spring. The Citizen's Patrol Corps was placed under the coordination of the mayor's office, under Harry Davis who was then executive director of the Urban Coalition. The operation was quite sophisticated as the corps was made up of four units. The North Side unit operated out of **The Way** under Dan Pothier; the second unit had the central area at TCOIC under a board member of **The Way** Joe Buckhalton; the third operated from Sabbathani Community Center covering the south side under Bill English. The fourth worked out of the Foshay Tower in downtown Minneapolis where the Rumor Control Center was located under the direction of Don Boyce. Volunteers who staffed the Rumor Control Center were trained to deal with misinformation that sweeps like a hot wind in moments of racial crisis. There were valuable things in this social experiment that became lost because the project was soon closed down when it appeared the crisis had passed. Though needed, Rumor Control was never used again. There is a fallacy in the method, if not madness, to always begin from scratch to meet each new crisis as if nothing had ever been learned.

After Dr. King's assassination in April 1968, there was more racial violence. Dan Pothier drew up a proposal for a citizens' patrol that would not drive cars but would walk the streets. It was originally called Corner Guards. The name was rejected for having negative connotations. It was Zev Aelony, a volunteer at **The Way**, who proposed the name Soul Force. Its purpose was to offer a street presence of restraint where there was potential violence. Its purpose was to represent a buffer zone between potential law-breakers and law-enforcers—both parties known for playing unfair and overstepping their boundaries.

The Soul Force enjoyed the support of the community. There was an incident where a Black person who lived in St. Paul harassed a member of the Soul Force. The kids from the North Side neighborhood took the side of the White Soul Force member; color was not the issue, the fact these White persons cared to be there on their behalf was what was important.

The Soul Force often kept trivial situations from blowing out of proportion. On one evening that summer, a car accident happened on

Plymouth Avenue. Two White Soul Force members, John Sherman, an International Relations student at Hamline University, and Robert Jamieson, first cellist with the Minnesota Orchestra, were on the corner of Penn and Plymouth Avenue when the accident occurred. A crowd gathered as an argument started. The White owner of Penn Del Café, who had the poor reputation in the neighborhood for standing armed outside his store at nights, came out with his revolver. Someone in the crowd grabbed the weapon and ran off with it. He angrily went back into his store and came out with a shotgun. Sherman and Jamieson got in front of the proprietor and stopped him from going anywhere. Soon the police arrived and took charge. A potentially violent scene was prevented. Here the Soul Force demonstrated what Ghandi originally meant by *satyagraha*, or "soul force," nonviolence is a greater truth than violence.[5] We can begin to appreciate the significance of the Soul Force and the extraordinary contribution it made by looking more closely at what continually transpires in the confrontation between the police and the Black community.

From the Scene to the Underlying Drama: 1968 Interview with James Baldwin

Kenneth Burke, literary critic and philosopher, offers an insight to the drama that underlines the ongoing conflict between police and the Black community. First let us examine Dr. Burke's proposition. He states, "Physical sciences are a calculus of events; the social sciences are a calculus of acts. And human affairs becomes dramatic criticism."[6]

Kenneth Burke is a wordsmith and a logician so we need to begin by looking at the different meanings of the word "calculus" Dr. Burke uses in two separate instances. Most of us know something about calculus. It is a method of calculation of higher mathematics. But not taking the class we don't know how to calculate using the symbols of calculus. Dr. Burke makes the claim *physical sciences* with the methodology of calculation and analysis of properties and their relationships are best equipped to present objective evidence. That is why the physical sciences are called in to calculate the various strands of evidence of a crime scene. Dr. Burke's proposition offers the telling clue to the conflict between police and the Black community. It is a potential crime scene where someone's civil rights will be violated or the human right to life will be taken.

Dr. Burke goes on to say the *social sciences* are equipped to make calculations of acts. The evidence of a crime scene doesn't necessarily address the question of why. Social sciences seek to understand human motives. The methodology of the social sciences is logical as it argues from a given hypothesis. Its argument gives us clues to what lies behind the act itself. In this case, the social sciences offer the motives that lurk behind the confrontation between police and the Black community. Social sciences show how violence is the fruit of such confrontations, the act that turns an event into a crime scene.

Yet with this knowledge of potential violence why does the confrontations between police and the Black community continue to take place? Dr. Burke's proposition makes the unusual claim that *dramatic criticism* can best provide us with an answer. In other words, to see the whole play of forces between police and the Black community we must see it enacted on an American stage.

Here the wordsmith changes his terms. The word "calculus" is replaced with the word "become." In philosophy this term is tied to ontology, the study of being. Human affairs is a history of becoming, human nature ever evolving and yet primordially caught by an ancient fault and flaw that produces murder. In biblical terms it is the story of Cain and Abel, the hand of violence raised against one's brother that marks humankind's progress. We can now add a third definition to the term calculus. It is a diseased condition and, like the stone itself, is galling to the human body and personality. It is the acidic accumulation of events and acts creating a chain of human dramas not welcomed nor anticipated, yet binding us tragically together.

James Baldwin offers the dramatic criticism of the novelist and the preacher in an interview with *Esquire*.[7] In Baldwin's telling, we are given a glimpse of the underlying drama that waits in ambush in every confrontation between police and the Black community. It has all happened before. It is a play where roles are assigned and though different actors come and go, the same action is always played out. Both the policeman and the Black cat from Harlem, Baldwin says, have seen it all before on television or in the movies. That is what makes everyone uptight and afraid. The policeman with his gun in his holster doesn't know the people it is his duty to protect anymore than the people know the cop on the beat. Ignorance is a frightful thing with a man who has a gun. If the policeman sees a Black cat out on the prowl after hours, he will stop him. It's his duty, it is his job to protect the community. But it is the Black cat's community and he doesn't like to be put down, put on front street, profiled, and classified as dangerous. Who is protecting whom here? And from what? Fear is the neighbor to anger. The Black cat says a word, raises his arm, the policeman strikes. Anger takes hold of the cat. Things are out of hand. A gun is fired and the Black cat falls. Like in the theater, if a gun is brought on stage, it will go off. The mark of violence, mark of Cain shows itself for what it is, an inheritance neither the policeman or the brother lying in the street can escape.

As a dramatic critic, Baldwin doesn't blame the policeman nor the Black cat for a poor performance. It is not simply their fault. In human affairs it is unbecoming of this country to cultivate such a lie. It is America that is to blame.

Who Will Advocate Before the Law for Ishmael?

The authority of government does not primarily come from the authority of law nor does it come from the authority of force. The authority of government rests in a democracy on the people, on the authority of the community itself. Laws, to be obeyed, must have the allegiance and support of the community. The community looks upon laws as corresponding to its conception of justice. We say the rule of law depends on the consent of the governed, and when that consent is not fully given, then the rule of law enforcement cannot take it back. The problem facing every Black community is they do not always believe the laws and the way laws are enforced correspond to their sense of justice. It is here where police power becomes a political liability. For where the body politic is in pieces, the arm of government, such as the police, cannot repair it. It is not that law and order are not wanted in the Black community; it is *whose version* of law and order that is being enforced.

The Way's Neighborhood Legal Complex

Today the Legal Rights Center in Minneapolis is a place Ishmaels can go to seek legal counsel and help. But in 1968, such advocacy was hard to come by. **The Way** sought to convince Black youths they could find an advocate they could trust. Working with Clyde Bellecourt from AIM (American Indian Movement) and a lawyer from the Dorsey legal firm, Syl Davis developed a proposal called A Neighborhood Legal Complex. Doug Hall, a lawyer, civil rights advocate, and a member of **The Way** board would later become the director of the Legal Rights Center.

The Neighborhood Legal Complex was organized to provide four things: [1] To see that persons charged with a crime under the present legal system get the best possible defense. [2] To change and improve the present system, to destroy the parts that discriminate against and persecute the individual. [3] To provide a means for youth participation in changing and improving the system. [4] To give the youth responsibility for organizing, staffing, and evaluating the work of the legal complex itself, so that it becomes their weapon against injustice and their defense against persecution.[8]

The Way's Neighborhood Legal Complex was an extraordinary effort to see the law protected and defended a person's rights. When one looks back at the struggle, it can only be said that people of color today need advocates for justice just as much as they did four decades ago. The case is drawn for a community advocate, like **The Way**, that can create the safety net for people who are falling through the cracks of society into oblivion.

The Veil of the Law

The need for advocacy is great as current legal interpretation of the law is hindered by the veil of thought that W.E.B. Du Bois so wisely articulated a hundred years ago in his instructive book *The Souls of Black Folks*. The insight Dr. Du Bois offered continually proves contemporary in its application and understanding of the need of persons of color before the law. Persons of color are born in a world that permits them to see themselves only through the eyes of others, others that view them with contempt and pity. A person of color is denied self-consciousness in such a world and must forever be on guard against the duplicity and fraud the other world would perpetrate on them. Dr. Du Bois writes, "One never ever feels his two-ness—reconciled strivings, two warring ideals in one dark body, whose dogged strength alone keeps it from being torn asunder."[9]

Dr. Robin Magee, Associate Professor of Law at Hamline University, views American jurisprudence as being veiled by such double-consciousness when it comes to judicial cases affecting persons of color. Cases of racial discrimination, such as racial profiling, must prove that race is the *sole* cause. Whereas cases such as affirmative action were reverse discrimination is charged, the law permits race to be used as the *predominant* cause in the debate over enrollment quotas based on race. Dr. Magee makes the startling observation that the latter is easier to prove than the first.[10] It is this deceitful double standard that reveals justice may be blind; yet the criminal justice system is proving all too often that persons of color, who expect justice, find themselves blindsided.

The Way and Minneapolis

Father Hennepin's Truth

The word Minneapolis comes from the combination of a Native American name for waters *[minne]* curiously combined with the Greek word for city *[polis]*. Minneapolis is a polis of the old world that sits precariously on a watery place in the new world. In the seventeenth century, Father Hennepin is the first European to come to this place. Here he comes to a waterfalls he names Saint Anthony after his patron saint. Hennepin, like the saint, views himself a captive to suffering. The American Indians had taken Hennepin captive. While worrying over his fate, the priest is given the opportunity to observe how his captors live. His writings are like Captain John Smith who is also captured and captivated by the Native Americans near Jamestown, Virginia. These Europeans are shrewd observers, interpreting what they see within their own cultural bias even as their observations often give way to moments of self-glorification.

The Jewish and Christian Bibles show a distrust for the city.[1] The first city is built by Cain, a murderer, who names the city after his son Enoch. Cain creates the art of craftsmanship. His bloody hands carve stones and thereby make the stones impure, unfit to build an altar for God. Yet Cain builds an altar demanding human sacrifice for the sake of keeping order in the city now lying outside the precinct of God's order of creation. Cain is in full assault against God. This is the motive behind naming the city Enoch, a name that means "initiation," to make and construct something new. The city is artificial, not natural, a new world opposed to creation; more, to supplant it.

The Dakota people lived in a place they called "blue tinted sky" long before Father Hennepin came in 1680. They knew the center of creation is at the fork of two rivers where the first human beings emerge from the earth. It is a place so holy no permanent dwellings can be built there. Their wisdom, like themselves, is discarded by the White Europeans who follow in the tracks of the missionary and adventurer Father Hennepin to settle in the land of many waters. They come to build and build they did—a garrison, a permanent fortification, later known as Fort Snelling, at the fork where the two rivers meet, the Mississippi and Minnesota. This place is called Mendota, the "Meeting of the Waters." The tainted legacy of Cain had come to the blue tinted sky country.

Stigma of Race and Place

Geography has everything to do with remembering and everything to do with **The Way. The Way** did not spring up in the suburbs; nor did it plant its feet in the dominant society, but in a community of dispossession. Ask anyone about the Near North Side in the mid-sixties and they would say it was a community where Jews and Blacks lived as if the fairly large White population who also lived on Near North Minneapolis did not exist. The word behind Jews and Blacks is race. Race and place, stigma and geography, go together just as acceptance and status go with a sense of place.

Early in the twentieth century the Near North Side of Minneapolis became the home of Ashkenazi Jews. These are the people who were nearly obliterated in the Nazi holocaust. The Ashkenazi Jews had lived for centuries in places that dotted the landscape, once called the Pale, in Central and Eastern Europe, the Baltic states, and the former Soviet Union. Today, one can still find on the Near North Side a large makeshift garage that once stabled a junk and rags wagon. The Ashkenazi were peddlers, peasants of the land, proletarian in spirit, and fundamental in faith. Unlike their richer and well placed cousins, the Sephardic Jews, who came earlier to Minneapolis from western Europe, they were orthodox in tradition and Messianic in their dreams. Americans have become acquainted with the Ashkenazi and their rich culture through the musical *Fiddler on the Roof*. Before coming to this country, Yiddish was their language before it gave over to English. These Jews were different. This is one of the first things to remember about the Near North Side.

Tex was getting on in age when I first met him. He was a storyteller. He loved to talk of the times he and other young Blacks hung out with their Jewish friends at North High School during the thirties and early forties. Those were the days when the Black community was living on the south side of Sixth Avenue that would be made over into Olson Highway [highway #55] in the 1950s, creating a corridor through the community for persons already seeking a way out of the city into suburbia and the countryside. Olson Highway is named after Floyd B. Olson, one of Minnesota's most popular governors who served during the Great Depression.[2] Today you can see a statue of Governor Olson looking north near Penn Avenue as it intersects highway #55. If you get close enough, you may see the governor's face masks a look of consternation. It is questionable whether the governor would have approved a highway dividing up his old neighborhood.

After the Second World War, Black folks began moving to the other side of Sixth into the Near North Side. Plymouth Avenue in those days was dotted with Jewish businesses, drugstores, bakeries, and haberdasheries. It all changed that night in early August 1966 when several Jewish establishments were destroyed by fire. Within eighteen months the prominent Bethel synagogue on Penn Avenue, just a block from Plymouth Avenue, voted to leave the Near North Side for a suburb known as St. Louis Park; other synagogues would soon follow. By 1968, nearly the entire Jewish community that once flourished in Near North Minneapolis, had made its exodus. The riots of 1966 and 1967 made the Near North community, in the public's mind, a Black community. Again, it is stigma of race that marks the place.

Blood Cements the City

People talk of downtown Minneapolis as center city. There is a building downtown called City Center. But the true center of the city is where there is an altar, where a living sacrifice is made. I do not speak of the Basilica or St. Mark's Cathedral, well known downtown churches, for their altars hold no sacrifices save in theological terms. The sacrifice I speak of is always one of blood, of blood cement. Since ancient times there has been a strong subliminal drive, no matter how disguised or excused, for sacrifice in maintaining order. Blood has been the cement in keeping society together. The principle of sacrifice and its use to maintain social order is understood today caught in the words of W. H. Auden's, "Cult of the Kill."

> *Here are the steps*
> *In the Iron Law of History*
> *That wields Order and Sacrifice:*

> *Order leads to Guilt*
> *(for who can keep commandments)*
> *Guilt needs Redemption*
> *(for who would not be cleansed!)*
> *Redemption needs Redeemers*
> *(which is to say, a Victim!)*

> *Order*
> *Through Guilt*
> *To Victimatge*
> *(hence: Cult of the Kill)*[3]

The ancient city's center was an altar.[4] The center of the city is a place of sacrifice, a place of murder. The founders of Rome were twins—Romulus and Remus, like Cain and Abel. Both Romulus and Cain killed their brothers before going on to build cities. "Cain went away from the presence of the Lord, and dwelt in the Land of Nod, east of Eden. . .and built a city, calling it after his son Enoch."[5]

Geographers know of no land of Nod. For it is a nowhere land, not a place but a lack of place. Cain no longer has a home, for murder has destroyed his home. He who builds cities is homeless seeking a home. The one who is homeless is condemned to the death of wandering. Those who build cities today do not live in them. They live in the "urbs," vacant moons that orb about the city. Those who have no home live in Nod, a land of sleep and wandering to and fro on congested arteries clotted with the many who travel alone. There is no center in this city of Cain that perpetuates the legacy of pillage, the endless pursuit of taking lives and property.

The deadly fruit of Cain's legacy is fear. Fear becomes real in the city. The first city was built as a rampart against outside threat. The divine command to Adam and Eve "to fill the earth and subdue it and have dominion over every living thing that moves upon the earth"[6] becomes in the hands of Cain's descendents a compulsion to order, to dominance, and control. And with domination comes anxiety. And in keeping with the curative role of victimage, someone needs to be blamed—the other becomes evil who is in league with the prince of disorder.

Truth is stranger than fiction, particularly if the fiction of a city is perpetuated on glossy promotional sheets and ad campaigns. A booster book on Minnesota carries the line, "This was a wild land, and the land held man in the cup of its hand; but now the land has been conquered. Now man can use the land as he will."[7] What comes across in every city's promotional pitch is that the city is forever seeking to remake its world over, though unbeknown to the reader, in Cain's image. The city, like Cain, sees itself building a sanctuary, a place free of danger; the city, like an oyster, continually develops a culture to absorb the pain of death's threats. The new myth of the city excludes the One who has power over life and death. The city kicks God out by reducing the divine to a hypothesis, marginalized, made superfluous and unreal.

The Angel of Minneapolis

The first time the word city is mentioned in the Bible, it appears as the Hebrew word "*iyr*" [meaning to guard or guardian angel]. The city has power, spiritual power in the form of a watching angel, it is a place of vigilance and terror.[8] The angel of Minneapolis, its spirit and identity, can be discerned. The clue is offered by the apostle Paul in his letter to the city of Colossi where he makes it clear city structures are simultaneously material and spiritual, one seen, the other unseen; one interior, the other exterior; one earthly, the other heavenly. They are the two poles of one reality. "For in [Christ] all things were created, in heaven and on earth, visible and invisible, whether thrones or dominions or principalities or authorities—all things were created through Christ and for Christ."[9]

Let us now embark on a first century social analysis by applying the political categories mentioned in the New Testament Book of Colossians to the city of Minneapolis.[10]

- The *throne* is the seat of power. The Greek word *thronos* appears over a hundred times in the Christian New Testament. Each time it refers to kings, dynasties, emphasizing the continuity and legitimacy of royal office. The throne in Minneapolis is occupied both by the mayor and the city council. Here incumbents come to sit before being forced out of office by popular vote, scandal, or by simply refusing to run for another term. The throne is the institutionalization of power in a set of symbols that includes the seal of office for the mayor as well as the city council that guarantee the city's continuity over time.

- *Dominion* is the realm or territory where the *kyrios* ruled. *Kyrios* is the Greek word for dominion. We may think of city limits. These are municipal boundaries such as the Mississippi River that is one of the few natural boundaries to the city, the others being marked off by streets before merging into the first ring of suburbs. Yet Minneapolis' dominion is much wider. Its social and political influence is felt throughout the metropolitan area that includes seven counties. Dominion consists of having the power to be the location for a new baseball stadium that once had its home in the suburb of Bloomington. Minneapolis nearly got its comeuppance as yet another baseball stadium is considered in the new millennium. The state legislature explicitly excludes Minneapolis, setting certain St. Paul legislators into rapturous delight naming St. Paul the site for the stadium. However, it proves to be of no avail. One can never count Minneapolis out. Such is the power of rule, of dominion.

- *Principality* is the prince or government. *Exousiai* is the Greek name for those in authority, those made legitimate; sanctioned with authority. It is the city council and its various committee structures that wheel and deal in their fashion offering favors or holding back their approval from certain quarters of self-interest. The Guthrie Theater almost did not have its way with city and state government. However, the Guthrie helped make a name for Minneapolis placing Minnesota on the cultural map. The city, no longer known as a "backwater" town, owes the princes of power a payback. Payback came when the Guthrie secured prime property near St. Anthony Falls to build its new theater. Such is the nature of powers behind the throne.

- *Authorities* is legitimization that comes with laws, taboos, mores, codes, and a constitution by which power is licensed along with the rituals, etiquette, and ideologies that enforce such power. This would include the courts, the police, election campaigns, press conferences, ground breaking, and photo opportunities, as well as the symbols of the city charter, the seal, billboards proclaiming city sponsorship for this development site, the mayor's image hung in the offices of underlings, etc.

There are other elements of spiritual power in Minneapolis. Food industries have been part of Minneapolis since its founding as flour mills were powered by hydroelectricity generated by Saint Anthony falls. Minneapolis also became a center for the medical industry at the University of Minnesota, located on the opposite bank of the Mississippi, providing competition to the Mayo brothers who developed innovative medical treatments in Rochester. The Mayo brothers' work became world famous. The provision of food and medicine influences life and death, thus holds spiritual power.

We can see the spiritual powers at work. The caduceus is the symbol for the medical profession; two snakes entwine around a staff. The cadmus illustrates the binary struggle of powers; one snake represents life, the other death. One example of this binary struggle is found in medicine in its use of chemotherapy. Here we have drugs that destroy not only cancer cells but also healthy cell tissue. Another example of the binary struggle of life and death is found in the way the food industry treats food products with various chemicals that make it possible to produce more food for a greater number of people. Yet the bind in the use of chemicals not only enhances a product, but also can endanger the health of individuals that consume these products as well as place the environment at risk.

So all powers, spiritually understood, have this binary bind. Drugs have their legal and illegal sides. The fact the commerce of illegal drugs is as global as any international corporate drug company, reveals how spiritual powers work both sides of the street. It follows then that the same rule of supply and demand that affect drug companies, and often manipulates prices, also rules illegal drug trade.

The political administration of the city council and mayor are entities that name only two distinct powers. The City of Minneapolis can be found in the telephone book, and with persistence, one eventually can contact some representative of the city. However, Minneapolis, the city, cannot be reached in the same way. One may say the mayor's office or the city council speaks for the city, but that is not quite true. The current administration is but one elected political manifestation of the city. There is also the school board and municipal judges that are elected, but neither speaks for the city, but rather only on issues regarding education and jurisprudence. There is civil service, another political manifestation that is never voted in or out of a job; patronage and budgets have sway in this world. Civil servants seldom can speak for the city, save in bars after hours. There is, of course, the chamber of commerce. But it does not speak for the city save, when it is in the interest of its business clients. Otherwise, should the city's interest be in conflict with its client's, then the chamber is nullified into silence. There is something much larger at stake. It is the spirit of the city and it has a long history that is never forgotten by the angel of the city.

So we come to the angel of Minneapolis. The term piques and intrigues. By it is meant the "inner spiritual reality" of the city. It is this identity and vocation, character and sense of purpose, we must come to understand and identify.

The idea is biblical. That the city is at the same time a human work and a spiritual power is key to understanding the work of principalities. Idolatry is the visible sign of the angel of Minneapolis. Today several buildings vie for being the tallest building in Minneapolis, and with that high distinction goes a sky tax. The Bible tells the story of the tower of Babel. "And they said to one another, 'Come, let us build ourselves a city, and a tower with its top in the heavens, and let us make a name for ourselves.'"[11] It is the city, not the tower, that is the center of the narrative. The notion of a tower means not so much reputation and notoriety as becoming independent, making its own name in the heavens. Today, it means the IDS or another competitor has to pay for having its head in the clouds. Why? It signifies dominion. It is a token of spiritual power. The city is not so much a Promethean act of rebellion reaching up to God as it is the act of making its own self-contained identity, creating its own urban environment, fulfilling its desire to be a great city. The biblical view is critical of such things seeing them as acts excluding God from creation. Such prideful efforts place trust in things that are not ultimate and in biblical terms such things make for idolatry.

Such is the fruit of Enoch—Babel, Babylon, Rome, Mexico City, Los Angeles, Paris, New York, and, alas, Minneapolis. This city seeks to emulate the big apple, as New York is fondly called, by calling itself the Minne-apple. [The Adam's apple reference, a legend and punning on the original temptation scene in Genesis, must be unconsciously, though ironically, justified.] Seeking meaning and justification by attaching the city's identity to New York City, trying to make it with a fallen angel, such pretension is met only by divine laughter. Mercifully God does not laugh at our aspirations.

To the Angel of Minneapolis Write This

An August night in 1966, that burst into fire on Plymouth Avenue, holds a revelation that still burns in the consciousness of some—a personal and political turning point. One could say this chapter is like the beginning of the Book of Revelation were Christ dictates letters to the angels of the churches. This essay could be titled "To the Angel of Minneapolis, Write This."

Where can we stand to listen to the voice that addresses the city? By the river's edge where Plymouth Avenue bridge crosses over the Mississippi River. Why here? A few years ago, Reverend Dr. James Forbes, senior minister at Riverside Church in New York City, came to Minneapolis in the cold of winter to speak at Augsburg College. He spoke to the city where a river runs through it. It is a reference to Minneapolis and the Mississippi River that runs through the city. It is also a reference to the river that runs through paradise in the Book of Revelation. Would it be here that we discern the angel of Minneapolis? Could it be here on the Plymouth Avenue bridge overlooking the Mississippi that the angel is to be addressed? Dr. Forbes, quoting the last chapter in the Christian Bible, the Book of Revelation's twenty-second chapter, speaks of a healing tree by the river that flows toward paradise whose leaves are the healing of the nations. He spoke a message that would bring healing to the nation. He spoke in a rapture of supposition: "Could Minneapolis be the place where God would do a new work? Was it not a city where a river runs though it? Could it be here the mark on the forehead of all the descendents of Cain will be erased with a new name? Could it be?"[12]

Fourteen years ago, Karen Stontag Satell, a local sculptor, working with foundry artists and community persons and students from North High School, created a piece of sculpture from handguns collected from "Drop Your Guns" program. The sculpture is called "Phoenix

Rising." It was placed in full view in the government center. In part, the sculpture was a creative response to the "Murder-Polis" image Minneapolis was being called. Like Cain's city, would Minneapolis be banished to a second rate city? Violence is the kernel of alienation that marks Cain; would it mark the brave new city of Minneapolis?

The sculpture is a marvelous conception that seeks to rename the angel of Minneapolis. Illegal guns were molded into a Phoenix rising out of the ashes of violence signaling a new spirit of peace. Not everyone welcomed the sculpture. Certain forces at the government center began to make it known they did not want the sculpture there. The angel of Minneapolis was putting up a fight; it was not ready to be changed into an angel of peace. The Greek ideal of the Phoenix sculpture hardly messed the feathers of the angel's wings, for it does not address the angel of Minneapolis as a spiritual power. The angel of Minneapolis has yet to be called back to its original source. The Christian Bible says that source is Christ.

Years before, I mentioned to Reverend Curtis Herron, pastor of Zion Baptist Church on the Near North Side that a peace sculpture should be placed outside the church. Zion, likes its namesake, sits on the brow of a hill overlooking Olson Highway and the surrounding city. Why a peace sculpture next to a church? The Christian proclamation that Christ is sovereign over all powers is made known by the church's critique of injustice and idolatry. Gun violence breeds injustice through the idolatry of force. Did not Jesus say those who pick up the sword will die by the sword? What better place for a symbol of peace than on the high promenade of a church hill? It would be a witness to the wisdom of the prophet Isaiah and the promise of peace that is offered by God: "They shall beat their swords into plowshares, and their spears into pruning hooks; nation shall not lift up sword against nation, neither shall they learn war any more."[13] A symbol of peace set on a hill for the rest of the world to see, particularly the world of crack houses sprinkled about the Near North Side as well as the world that hurries by on the other side.

The crack houses are like the "blind pig" of Prohibition days with its tavern culture where diverse and illicit services are often the place of set-ups, places of fencing operations that exchange cocaine for stolen goods; all of them arsenals full of weapons. Around crack houses you can almost taste the acrid smell as one walks across the shadow of death. Reverend Jerry McAfee and his congregation have gone to stand in front of crack houses, publicly calling out the demon that holds court in such damned places. Their liturgies of exorcism are a discernment of death and a public rebuke. Their cries to God are a way to set at liberty neighborhoods, indeed make the city of Minneapolis and its angel free. Another witness and public rebuke will come when someone places these startling words on the Phoenix sculpture, now exiled outside of the government center, "A Message to the Spirit of Minneapolis from the One who was Dead but Now Lives." Should one do this, they would probably be arrested just as another was arrested in another city in another time. Such is the nature of the times, such is the nature of powers.

Jesus approaches Jerusalem. He looks over the city and says, "Would that you even today knew the things that make for peace."[14] Jerusalem bears ironically the name city of peace. Jesus discerns the angel of Jerusalem and spoke directly to it. Jesus could see the powers and the economic weight of the city on the people. Jesus would oppose the interests of the Temple, its obligations, its restrictions on the poor. It is then Jesus spoke of his love for the city: "O Jerusalem, Jerusalem, killing the prophets and stoning those who are sent to you!"[15]

There is an agonized love here that causes Jesus to break down in tears, even as he approaches the city to confront and rebuke its power. Possibly, love for the city is a prerequisite to discernment. It is certainly true Jesus hoped Jerusalem could recognize its own karios, its own spiritual meaning. **The Way** sought to hold up such hope for the reclaimable meaning of justice. Tragically, it was largely shunned and pushed aside and now nearly forgotten. The struggle goes on. We have much to learn and possibly one day we can teach the angel of Minneapolis what it too must yet learn.

The Way and The Media

A mirror has no heart but plenty of ideas.

—Malcolm De Chazal [1]

Mass Media: The Mirror that has Plenty of Ideas

The hidden danger of mass media is that it acts like a mirror, pulling a person into its image. Lost in the mirror, bereft of oneself, the self has no thoughts, no reflections save the reflection in the glass. Media acts like a watery glass that refracts images and bends them to its own shape. The image becomes the reality. To quote Hertz' law, "The consequences of the images will be the images of the consequences."

The consequence of societal images projected on one as talented as Claude Brown can be devastating as the author distorts reality in his vain effort to play to the crowd. Albert Murray, the insightful man from Harlem, said as much in his critique of Brown's *Manchild in a Promised Land.* He called it an autobiographical social science fiction that is popular with White readers. However Black readers won't stay up late reading the latest gossip about themselves nor give much credit to books that tell dirty stories about Black folks that White folks can listen in on.

Murray's devastating critique of Brown and his book when it first appeared in 1965 was offered in the hope the young writer would one day outgrow his need to be the "mass media Negro" spokesman. Murray saw the danger in the media's manipulation of one into being a mouthpiece, an entertainer who will make a sizeable income and keep himself in the spotlight as long as one writes the kind of things that pleases White people.

Albert Murray understands the manipulation of the media at the service of the dominant society. Its attendant power to oppress people by impressing them they are something they are not. Murray identified this media hype as the White hunter on safari looking for, as he called it, "an expert on U.S. jungle manners and mores" where natives are no longer called savages but "culturally deprived."[2] It meant the same thing but the sociological language was a way to fool folks into thinking things were different. It was about self-promotion at the expense of others by placing them in the pocket where the eight ball is headed. It is a dangerous game were the prey can turn to stalk the hunter. Albert Murray's point about media is simple enough—living out the entertainment requirements of safari.

Near North Minneapolis: The Unlikely Image

The media plays to the sensational side of Near North Minneapolis. These images reveal only a small part of the actual texture of their varied lives. Here are people who inhabit a complex and endlessly fascinating part of the city. The media dwells, more often than not, on the pathological and the documentary proofs of a world that is other than the world of the viewer or reader. It is the liabilities of Near North Minneapolis that is often referred to on cue. The cue could be the anniversary of the riot on Plymouth Avenue or the latest homicide or shootout with the police. Whatever the cue, the conclusion is the same, the Near North Side is a dangerous community.

Even the naming of boulevards can become political liabilities. A boulevard that runs from downtown Minneapolis into Near North Minneapolis, linking White and Black worlds, is named for Van White, a former Black city councilman. Mr. White, in his tenure as councilman, garnered the respect for his work on behalf of his constituents. The naming of the Van White boulevard is well deserved. However, the telling fact is he won approval over Earl Craig, a Black man that had established a reputation as the head of the Urban Coalition and who gained notoriety by running for the senate against a famous White Minnesotan, Hubert Humphrey. However, it is the tragic circumstances surrounding his death that disqualified Earl Craig from having a memorial boulevard named after him. A gay male, in a liaison he frequently sought, murdered him. Being Black and homosexual is to be doubly ostracized. In the Black community the first image causes anger; in some quarters the second image provokes condemnation of one of their own.

The media sews a seamless straight jacket offering the impression that nothing in Near North Minneapolis has changed for the better. It reports there are not enough jobs, which leads many to crime. Crime and profit are the tainted fruit of a thriving drug business, one of the largest capitalistic ventures in any community of oppression. The media offers little to counter the stereotypical images of the ghetto [a term for European enclaves forced upon Jews] that associate images of poverty with Black powerlessness and gang warfare along with Black self-hatred.

When the media looks at Near North Minneapolis, it largely sees criminals and addicts. But this is not the picture the community has of itself. Few communities could claim to have musicians who played with famous jazz bands living next door to former Viking football players, as well as well-known politicians, teachers, lawyers, and preachers. Here the rich and the poor, the powerful and the weak, live side by side and think it is as normal as the sunrise in the morning. The media reports that people are out of jobs but fails to show that opportunities to make a living are not given to every person. Lack of jobs turns out to be the biggest thief in Near North Minneapolis. The camera needs to be pointed in that direction, not at an empty lot or the empty life of an addict. Emptiness may be human, but it is not what humans seek unless circumstance, temperament, or a dream deceived them.

Near North Side may be a social worker's dream, but that is because people who live elsewhere totally misunderstand the vibrant community that exists here as a prism of cultures. Here people are shrewd urbanites who carry with them the long standing patience that knows nothing comes without a struggle, nothing is free without a price, nothing of value is given without something of value being sacrificed.

Media Becomes Evidence: Police Riot on Plymouth Avenue

Things have changed since the sixties. Now civilians have cam recorders to video record events such as the police beating Rodney King in Los Angeles. People are no longer totally dependent on the news media for what really happened. However, a rare reporting event took place in August 1969. Molly Ivins, now a nationally syndicated columnist with Creators Syndicate known for "telling it like it is," in 1969 was a *Minneapolis Tribune* staff writer who reported a police riot.

Molly Ivins was on the Near North Side when a police riot took place, and she unflinchingly describes it as such. Her article appeared nearly two weeks after the confrontation, under the headline "Profile of Confrontation: How It Was on North Side."[3] Her report was prefaced with editorial commentary that sought to downplay what took place.

The events recorded were the nights of August 12 and 13. She witnessed confrontations between Minneapolis police and people along Plymouth Avenue. No one was hurt severely and no property was destroyed. Some would have thought it an unremarkable example of the police-minority brushes that were happening with great frequency in many cities in the late sixties. What is unremarkable was the police riot. What is remarkable is the reporting by Molly Ivins in spite of editorial misinformation. Her article offers a blow by blow report that confirms the evidence of a police riot.

She describes the scene looking like a miniature replay of the 1968 Chicago Democratic Convention. Crowds taunting, police charging, the scream of civilians caught in the charge, riot sticks rising and coming down, the thud of kicks on a body—sensed rather than heard.

It starts innocently around 9:00 p.m. on Tuesday evening as people stood around on the corner of Plymouth and Queen Avenues. The group welcomes several persons who had come from a meeting of the Citizens Community Centers. They gather in front of the G&K Grocery and Letofsky's Delicatessen, both closed and the site of recent picketing by a group that called itself Independent Coalition of Blacks. Things had not gone well at the Citizen Center meeting. The federal government had ordered a cut off of CCC funds. The talk on the corner hashed over the federal cut-off of CCC funds.

By 10:30 p.m. the crowd had grown to about one hundred persons. Squad cars converged on the area about 11:00 p.m. after the police radio carried a report of rock-throwing. The crowd told the fifty policemen who came in riot gear they didn't know anything about throwing rocks. Matthew Eubanks, the CCC director, spoke with Deputy Inspector Edwin Schonnessen. Eubanks wondered why the show of force to a peaceful gathering of community people unless the police wanted to provoke a riot. Schonnessen said that the police had not come to provoke anyone but to protect them. "From what?" asked Eubanks.

At 12:15 a.m. Wednesday, Schonnessen announced over a bullhorn that the crowd was blocking traffic and needed to disperse. Persons in the crowd wondered what traffic? Some booed as they began their trek eastward on Plymouth Avenue toward **The Way** followed closely by a police phalanx in measured step.

Ivins reported that at 12:22 a.m. the police lines stop as the crowd had moved three blocks to the intersection of Plymouth and Morgan. Suddenly the shout went out "Charge!" The police rushed the crowd and the people scattered. End of night one.

The following night at 10:00 p.m. things begin to take on a familiar shape. A crowd of fewer than a hundred gather at the same corner of Plymouth and Queen for a free barbecue provided by Dr. Tom Johnson on the lawn and sidewalk in front of his clinic. A flyer circulated the community earlier in the day announcing a rally. Some came out of curiosity, others to see if the police would show, and still others who were angry about the previous evening.

By 11:30 p.m. the crowd grew to over a hundred. Matt Eubanks arrives with Earthia Wiley, administrator of the South Side CCC, from a stormy CCC board meeting. At 12:15 a.m. Thursday, Eubanks and Wiley, along with Gene Lewis and Wes Hayden, appear on top of the roof between Letofsky's and G&K to talk to the crowd. They urge the crowd across the street at the barbecue to come closer. Crowd spills out into the street. Ivins and other reporters counted just seven cars over the next fifteen minutes that had to slow down to get past the crowd. There was no trouble with anyone in the cars or with the people who had gathered in the street.

It is 12:30 a.m. as nearly seventy police in full riot gear, along with plain clothes men, appear on Plymouth to the west of the crowd. The police form two semi-circular lines. People begin drifting away down side streets. Eubanks cries out to them to stay put and stick together. "It is your community. You are doing nothing wrong."

The familiar voice of Schonnessen declares over his bullhorn they are an unlawful assembly and must disperse in two minutes. Catcalls are heard. "You gonna move two hundred people in two minutes? I'm gonna stick around to see you try." Schonnessen repeats the order two more times. The crowd again begins moving east toward **The Way** as it did the night before.

At 12:33 a.m. it begins again. Dejavu—the same voice, same taunts, same heavy feet marching in step, same order. Bryant Page, 2705 11th Avenue South, father of seven and an employee of Minneapolis-Moline, is walking away from the crowd when he begins screaming. "How can we be an unlawful assembly, for God's sake? We're moving, we're walking, we're obeying, we're not assembled anywhere!" Later Page said, "I guess I was having a fit of bewilderment or insanity. Seems like you see the police doing this all over the world and then to see it right here. There was a time when I could have ignored that thing but something inside me snapped." As the police lines pass Penn and Plymouth, Schonnessen calls out, "Go get that loudmouth." Two policemen arrest Page without violence in front of his car. He is charged with unlawful assembly, shouting obscenities, and blocking traffic.

It is 1:00 a.m. The police line again halts at the Morgan intersection as it had done the night before. But this night the crowd scrambles into the open door of **The Way**. Eubanks urges people to get inside, off the street. There is a jam at the door. People who get inside stand to look out and unwittingly block the door for others to come in. There are still thirty people caught outside when Schonnessen cries out, "We've been patient long enough," and signals to police squad leaders to give the order to charge. Molly Ivins vividly reports the scene, "Again the military-attack yell, the shoes pounding the pavement, screaming, panic, sudden jamming into **The Way**, people pushing over one another, knocking down a child."

Wes Hayden and Mel Dillion return after they went looking for a small group of children told to be frightened and crying, cut off on a side street. They hadn't found them. Arriving at **The Way's** entrance Hayden sees the crowd cramming into the building with police charging. He said later all he did was uncross his arms. Police sticks start to come down. Hayden's beret flies along with his glasses. Five officers stand over him as he falls to his knees. The article reports there are bruises all over his torso. Mel Dillion, on the other side of **The Way's** door, throws a punch at one of six or seven policemen surrounding him. Police sticks come down on his head until he falls. Several reporters witness Dillion being kicked several times as he lies on the pavement.

Besides Wes Hayden and Mel Dillion, several others were arrested. Vickey Smiley, 18, 1223 Newton Avenue North, tries to run, but a policeman grabs her hair rollers and she is dragged to a paddy wagon. Of those arrested, three are White.

The police riot is caught on film taken by WCCO-TV reporter on the scene. I secured the film, as president of the board of **The Way,** from WCCO-TV through the kind office of the president of Midwest Radio-Television, Van Konynenburg. Video evidence of the police riot is shown by **The Way** staff to board members and persons of the community who are appreciative **The Way** was open to serve as a sanctuary from the police.

Nearly a hundred people stayed in the basement of **The Way** until 3:30 a.m. that morning talking, venting their frustration and anger. Mrs. Ruby Barber, a member of the CCC board and ordinarily a quiet woman, couldn't keep back her rage. "They had a lawyer man up there, did you see it? [Reis Mitchel, police attorney.] They brought him up especially and he had to hunt through all his law books for an hour to find some tiny, stupid law they could say we were breaking. Waited long enough, they could've arrested us all for spitting on the sidewalk. Oh, that lawyer man would have found something." The article ends as Schonnessen nonchalantly saying he didn't feel there was brutality or overuse of force. He gave the order, he said—gave the warning many times. He did it according to the rules.

The cut-off of CCC funding, Molly Ivins reported, that was the initial conversation the first night people gathered on Plymouth Avenue has its own Minnesota connection. The suspension of CCC funding came on the orders of Don Rumsfeld, who seems to have worked most of his adult life inside the beltway, then head of OEO (Office of Economic Opportunity) under Nixon. The closing down of the CCC program came on the heels of complaints by Minnesota Congressman Clark MacGregor. The congressman would later have his name tainted for his part in the Watergate scandal. MacGregor had talked to Alan Beals, Chicago regional OEO director. The congressman told the *Star* that he was told "in effect" by Beals that Matthew Eubanks, Earthia Wiley, and Edgar Pillow "have to go." The *Star* went on to report MacGregor is an old friend of Rumsfeld and had talked with him about events leading up to the suspension of CCC funds. The congressman had gone on record for the administration as saying "the whole thing is going to go down the drain if the Blackstone Rangers [a Chicago gang] and the Matt Eubankses take control of every city."[4] Molly Ivins' courageous reporting of a police riot on Plymouth Avenue made it clear who was in control of Minneapolis.

Making News or Being Made Over by the News

The question really is why don't we want to air dirty laundry?
That's because of the fact that we know from our past experiences
that most folks don't see it as dirty laundry.
They see it as the entirety of our clothing—
it's always dirty and always bad.
The American and European media, who control the images we see,
expose things from a perspective that is not in sync
with fulfilling the needs of and respecting our community.
We still live in a racist society,
and we tend to give ammunition to those who would use it against us
while we are trying to stop small groups of folk
from doing further damage internally.

—Vusmusi Zulu[5]

The Way appeared in the news media frequently in those early years. What made news and what did not is what is most revealing. One of the hot stories that wasn't so cool was the story regarding Syl Davis' arrest.

Excerpts that follow of Syl's arrest, charge, and trial, charges later dismissed, are taken from the *Minneapolis Star* and *Tribune* newspapers. [The *Star* was the evening paper and the *Tribune* was the morning edition; both newspapers in 1970 were owned by the same company.] Though the events took place in St. Louis, Missouri, Twin City readership at the time would have generally known about **The Way** and so would be interested in the controversy surrounding its director.

SYL DAVIS CHARGED ON MARIJUANA COUNT is the headline for the *Star* article dated May 1, 1970. It reports Sylvester Davis, the director of **The Way**, had been charged with illegal possession of marijuana following his arrest in St. Louis. It also mentions a Benjamin F. Bell was in Syl's car when it was stopped for a traffic violation. The police found a .38 caliber revolver, a .22 caliber pistol, a tape recorder, and a movie camera, along with marijuana and hashish. The article goes on to report no decision had been made on whether the two men would be returned to Indiana because the .38 revolver had been stolen in Indiana.

What is not said in this article? Who is Benjamin Bell? And where is he from? It turns out that Mr. Bell ran a similar program like **The Way** in Indianapolis and was traveling with Syl to visit other centers. The fact the gun was stolen in Indianapolis does throw some suspicion toward Mr. Bell. But no mention of Bell's connection to Indianapolis is made. There is also the pending decision to have them both sent to Indiana, implying Syl Davis was possibly implicated in a gun theft.

The next day headline in the *Star* read SYL DAVIS OUT ON $1,700 BOND. Again, Syl is identified as the director of **The Way**. The article states he was released on charges of illegal possession of marijuana as well as an improperly lighted license plate.

We now see why the police stopped Syl's car. His license plate did not have a light, common to cars bought in other states that do not require such things, however, a liability as one drives out of East St. Louis, a predominant African-American community, into St. Louis. The discerning reader must ask what happened to Mr. Bell? Was there not a gun stolen from Indiana?

Tribune headline for June 10, **THE WAY** HEAD BOUND OVER FOR MARIJUANA TRIAL. Syl's attorney, hired by **The Way**, argued in a preliminary hearing in St. Louis criminal corrections that Syl Davis' arrest and subsequent search of his car that led to the narcotics charge, stemming from a minor traffic violation, was unlawful. The court disagreed saying there was "probable cause" to bind Mr. Davis over to circuit court for trial. Today, such stop and search is called "racial profiling."

DAVIS PLEADS INNOCENT TO DRUG CHARGE is the *Tribune's* June 19 headline. The trial date is set for September 21. In this article we read for the first time what happened to Benjamin F. Bell who is now identified as a resident of Indianapolis, Indiana. He was jailed, along with Syl, and later released, unlike Syl, without being charged.

Again, one must ask whatever happened to the stolen gun charge? Since the first article, there is no mention of the stolen gun from Indiana. If one had not been following these articles this small bit of information would be easily overlooked.

On November 13, the *Tribune* headline read MOTION MADE FOR DISMISSAL IN DAVIS CASE. The article indicates Syl Davis as the former director of **The Way.** Syl had resigned on October 2, a little over four years after being named **The Way's** first director. The article focuses on the reason for dismissal. Syl's attorney, Norman London, based his motion for dismissal on a recent decision by the Missouri Supreme Court that reversed a lower court conviction of a similar case. That case involved a man who was charged for marijuana possession. The evidence, as it was in Syl's case, was seized by the police upon a search of his car. The high court ruled such a search was illegal and was nothing more than a "fishing expedition."

SYL DAVIS ACQUITTED OF DRUG CHARGE was the *Tribune's* final article on December 1, 1970, over seven months after Syl's initial arrest. The circuit judge acquitted Syl Davis on a charge of illegal possession of marijuana. The judge said the November 9 Missouri Supreme Court ruling did in fact apply to Mr. Davis' case. The judge went on to say, "there were no facts in evidence upon which anyone could believe the officer was in any danger from the contents of the car."

Syl Davis had won, but the damage to his reputation had already been done. No newspaper board of review would criticize the *Star* and the *Tribune's* reporting of Syl Davis arrest, charge, and trial. Beyond that is the fact there were no other voices raised on his behalf, save the board of **The Way.** No African-American newspaper in the Twin Cities took up Mr. Davis' case to provide another perspective. The Black media's failure to give Syl Davis a full public hearing meant it abandoned one of its own significant voices.

The Other Side that Didn't Make the News

The Way board of directors sought to correct the negative image among its contributors projected on to Syl Davis and, in turn, on **The Way** itself. One only had to read the headline "'The Way' Head Bound Over for Marijuana Charge" to know that more than Syl was on trial. Syl Davis was on trial, but so was **The Way** in the minds of most persons reading those articles. The charges against Syl may have been dismissed, but his resignation simply confirmed in many people's minds that he was guilty.

The Way board pulled no punches in its counter attack. It immediately sent out the following news release.

> Publicity surrounding the event has been brutal. If a design existed to damage **The Way,** it could not have been pursued more effectively than this was. As you know, it comes in the midst of our annual campaign for funds to keep **The Way's** programs going. There is hope, of course, that the charges will be dropped. All circumstances of the affair are being investigated by attorneys and others. Meanwhile, **The Way** has suffered badly in the judgment of many.[6]

The directors rallied to Syl Davis' defense to offer its side of an event that would otherwise never be reported.

> Syl denies having possession of marijuana. There are a number of reasons for believing that a small brown envelope police claim to have found in Syl's car, and the fact that they stopped him and searched in the first place, were part of a pattern of harassment he experienced several times during two weeks of driving across the country. Syl was on a much-needed vacation (his first in nearly four years at **The Way**). He had visited several cities—Chicago, Toledo, Pittsburgh, Philadelphia, and others—to check with friends in each one on local poverty and minority programs. In the process, he had been stopped several times by police (twice by state patrolmen within thirty miles) and searched thoroughly—even to

the lining of his clothes and a telephone check with his doctor in Minneapolis on some prescription pills he had. Nothing illegal was found. We find it impossible to believe that any person with the experience, and with good reasons to believe he was under constant police surveillance, would be likely to cruise into St. Louis with a packet of narcotics practically in plain view. (He was stopped by two officers of a special detachment supposedly because of a faulty license light. While Syl was questioned at the patrol car by one, the other officer returned from Syl's car within a minute or two claiming to have found the envelope which he said contained marijuana. Contents were shown to Syl. Other things belonging to Syl, including a tape recorder and camera, were confiscated and held by the police.) As incredible as this seems to most of us, Black persons associated with **The Way** insist that they are not surprised, that it is but another example of the kind of treatment they experience almost routinely.[7]

No News is Good News: Image of the Consequence is the Consequence of the Image

There ain't no more hot summer and the niggers ain't gonna raise no more hell. So we don't need **The Way** *no more.*

—Frank Alsop[8]

It's the same old story.
When the rocks were flying, the money was coming in.
When the rocks diminished, so did the money.

—Edgar D. Pillow[9]

The Way was going broke. A newspaper article on **The Way's** troubles appeared two days after Syl Davis announced his resignation under the headline, "What Undermines **The Way**?" The article is an eulogy and like all eulogies it is time to set the record straight.

The Way was unique in modern Minneapolis history. More than any other community agency, it was created through an alliance between a Black community beset by violence in the summer of 1966 and influential leaders who had the wealth and power to channel money into a venture for self-determination.[10]

Private contributions, by the time Syl announced his resignation in early October, were down by $88,000 when compared to the previous year. A reduced staff kept the doors open. The newspaper article offered a list of reasons for the loss of funds—**The Way** was a center of agitation; **The Way's** image was damaged by Director Davis' arrest on possession of marijuana; **The Way** had failed in its mission to unite the community in broad neighborhood development; corporations only gave one-time seed gifts and that fund-raising, according to one unidentified corporate leader, was not as aggressive as it had been.

One must remember that **The Way**, in these early years, did not seek public funding. So the fund-raisers, knowing how important private funds were to the work of **The Way**, were relentless as they went in person, time and time again, year in and year out, seeking funds from whomever would hear them out. They did it with little thanks and were often criticized for supporting **The Way**. But that did not stop them. Even though this thank you comes late, to all the fundraisers I say, Bravo! A small handful of board members such as Ray Plank, Sage Cowles, Penny Winton, Gordon Ritz, along with a few others, nearly raised all the money single-handedly. And there was no one better, more determined, and able in raising money as well as raising issues than Louise McCannel.

The corporate leader who said that fund-raising was not aggressive knew that he [most likely a he] was smart to keep his name out of the paper; otherwise, he would have to contend with Louise McCannel who knew most of the power elite by name, if not by reputation. Louise was unafraid. Some Black folks claimed that they were "tellin' it like it is" but few laid it on the line like Louise. Here is an excerpt of a letter that was mailed to potential donors. A letter that some on the board, Black and White members alike, said was too strong. You judge for yourself. I believe Louise knew how to address power.

There are reasons, which need not be analyzed here, why this large number of people [the poor and the Black poor] has been barred from community opportunity systems, and why, except in a negative way, this group has been almost completely ignored by those who control the decision-making machinery. Suffice it to say that these citizens at the bottom of the economic, social, and cultural ladder can no longer be kept out of sight and out of mind by the larger community. They *will* be heard, either as another community group jockeying with traditional methods for a share of community benefits and opportunities, or as rebels protesting with a variety of disruptive means against continued discrimination and exclusion.

Traditional programs mostly attract clients who are already middle class oriented. The type of citizen served by **The Way**, whether rightly or wrongly, distrusts so profoundly those in charge of these traditional programs that they will have nothing to do with them if they can help it.

To expect the personal staffing such programs to change their attitudes and methods sufficiently to suddenly attract this alienated segment of our population is about as reasonable as expecting Goldwater Republicans to start behaving in a manner likely to recruit Norman Thomas Socialists.

On the other hand, to expect these previously excluded poor to sit quietly back until the community power structure is ready to move over and allow them to participate in making community decisions is roughly as likely as expecting a business firm to wait patiently for its profits until its competitors decide how much territory shall be assigned to it.

To predict that without **The Way** there will be renewed violence on the North Side may seem to some a kind of blackmail instead of what it is, a conclusion arrived at from common knowledge about human behavior. It is neither blackmail nor a dazzling feat of prophecy to predict that there will be violence on the South Side, probably this summer, because so far all efforts to forestall it are again based on the traditional philosophy and methods which did not prevent last August's Plymouth Avenue disturbance.

Those who believe that **The Way** itself is a product of violence-as-blackmail forget the preceding weeks when, as seen by the attached clippings, there were those who knew that jobs for North Side youth, for example, would be a critical factor in preventing the buildup of frustration and bitterness. Such feelings produce an ambience conducive to violence, just as certain climatological conditions indicate tornado possibilities, causing the weatherman to proclaim a "tornado alert." (On the South Side today there is a "violence alert.")

A community has only two basic choices in response to the kind of violence which boiled over on Plymouth Avenue last August: counter-violence in the form of a police crackdown, which, in its turn, usually produces an escalation of violence on both sides; or a serious community effort to meet the needs that such outbreaks indicate. That Minneapolis chose the latter course is a credit to its collective good sense, and provides hope that community leaders will see that such efforts must be continued if the root causes, as well as the violent symptoms of alienation in North Side Minneapolis (as well as in other areas), are to be removed.[11]

These persons on the board carried off an impressive fund-raising effort. Beginning in 1966—$56,790.64 was raised from 76 contributions in four short months; in 1967—$111,134.28 was raised from 446 contributions; and 1968—$187,000 was received from more than 800 contributions. By mid-summer 1970, after four years of fund-raising, more than half a million dollars had been raised from over two thousand contributions, ranging from a few pennies to many thousands of dollars from individuals, foundations, businesses, religious groups, and other non-governmental sources. I am sure few, if any other community organizations in the Twin Cities over a similar stretch of time, had the same success in fund-raising. Success is hardly the word, miraculous would be closer to what a few dedicated people achieved. In terms of twenty-first century monies, a handful of people raised, solely from private sources, what would amount today to over two million dollars. Factor in the controversy that surrounded **The Way,** and you begin to sense the extraordinary feat these persons accomplished. Such was the commitment that lie behind the high promise of those days.

Even so, by 1970, **The Way** was never able to generate funds more than a month or two ahead of the bills. Soon contributions were coming in after the bills. There was a staff misunderstanding about an expected contribution. As a result, payroll checks were bouncing all over town, alarming one creditor, Northwestern Bell Telephone, so the company shut off telephone service well before the end of the usual grace period. Having no telephone service disturbed more creditors, as well as alarming persons in the community that **The Way** is shutting down.

The Way had gone through many crises, but this time it was different. Syl Davis told the board in August 1970, that he would resign as director effective November first. When Syl publicly announced his resignation in early October there was a deep resignation in his words.

> In 1966, we started a job of trying to bring an awareness and some community movement toward self-determination for the people who had been left out. We envisioned that certain specific needs existed within the community, and we have seen some of those needs come to pass. We provided leadership in a community that had lacked movements or even aspired to change of any form. My point is that what is done cannot be undone very easily. And we cannot rest on laurels. It is with this thought that I feel we must make significant changes lest we become a part of that which we have fought— "established."[12]

There was such heaviness in that last sentence, an exhaustion of spirit that had not only came on Syl but also others on the staff and board who had fought for four long years against immeasurable powers of resistance to social change; more, sought a change of heart that is the yearning seat for justice.

In October, when Syl Davis' resignation was made known, the sense of resignation had come upon many board members. Key board members had already resigned and more followed. Some were burnt out from the demand of continual fund raising, some for being on a board that continually dealt with issues demanding a resolve to live with the unresolvable; still others believed that whatever the future held for **The Way**, without Syl Davis' leadership it would be an organization they could not wholeheartedly support.

With Syl Davis' departure, a vacuum developed that attracted several proposals. **The Way** board was not ready to name a new director without funds to support new programs. The organization Black Thoughts, led by Harry "Spike" Moss, who was one of the original young men on the staff of **The Way**, proposed to become the new staff and take over its program. The board rejected their proposal but left it open for them to buy the building and use their own name. The organization did not have those kinds of funds and so the proposal went by the way side. Spike Moss did not sit idly by. He would later make it clear at a board meeting in 1972 that he would be a major player in **The New Way**. He soon gained a reputation in working out community disputes with the police, a role he continues to this day. By 1974 Spike Moss had taken over the directorship.

Another option was selling the building to the Housing Authority, which had expressed interest in buying the building. The Housing Authority would pay off the mortgage with the remaining balance of $14,000 going to **The Way** Laboratory School under the leadership of Gwyn Jones-Davis (former Program Director of **The Way**) that had recently become the occupants of a building on Olson Highway. However, it turned out that it would take much longer than previously thought to negotiate a sale. With little or no funds, the board was faced with the painful decision of closing the building.

It was then that Bert Davis, the assistant administrator of **The Way**, offered three important facts. [1] The young people in the neighborhood felt the building was their building, and if it closes, they could only see it as something more being taken away from them. [2] If the building can ever be sold, there must be something to negotiate with. A closed building deteriorates and could be subject to vandalism. [3] The staff had received a number of letters and visits from people in the community who expressed their dismay at the prospect of losing **The Way**. These facts before them, the board resolved to keep the building open until March 15, 1971, and Bert Davis be named the interim director with the understanding he would lead a fund drive asking for $5 pledges for three years from 40,000 businesses in the metropolitan area.

By the end of 1971, there were few $5 pledges from 40,000 businesses, but Bert Davis had given **The New Way** a make over. In his words, **The New Way** would no longer be a "Black-oriented thing," as its programs would reflect a more traditional community center. Bert also initiated discussions with the United Way. At a meeting of the board, a significant question was asked of Russ Ewald, who had come to represent the United Way. "Why was **The Way** not funded by the United Way before?" Reverend Ewald offered the following reason: "The guidelines were too strict at that time, but the guidelines have changed, as well as **The New Way's** outlook and activities, and we are more qualified now than we were at that time." It is a curious response. The "we" hardly refers to the United Way though it is implied. The "we" really referred to the new administration at **The New Way**. "Qualified" in this context was a clear signal the powers to be were accepting **The New Way** into the fold of the United Way. Bert Davis put it to the board "either join or close."[13]

Syl Davis' warning that there was danger in becoming "established" went unheeded. **The New Way** had become part of the establishment. The price came high, bringing to an end a extraordinary experiment that brought the poor and rich together in a common pursuit that in itself was part of an infant beginning to an act of liberation. For a moment we had **The Way**.

The Way
and The Black Church

The Way and Black Folk Religion

The Way supported the power values of the Black Church, though the Black churches in the Twin Cities did not necessarily support **The Way**. As **The Way** openly associated itself with Black Power so it set itself at odds with Black churches; ironically, it was this very espousal of power that is the heart of Black Folk Religion.

Black Folk Religion is centered about the Bible. The Book of Exodus holds a key biblical story that proclaims, "Let My People Go." It is a liberation story of slaves being freed from Egyptian bondage by a God whose power is greater than the ruling master Pharaoh. Power is key to the story of freedom, for powerless people are not free in this world. The Bible stories of slaves becoming a nation of free people in a Promised Land has always resonated in the lives of those whose kinfolk were once slaves in this New Canaan land, these United States. With this background one can better understand how power takes on a special significance for Black Folk Religion. Power means life from God and, in its exercise, to do the things necessary to meet the needs of the community.

The Way reasserted the use of power in meeting the needs of the community that was a central tenet of Black Folk Religion; yet, to its surprise, **The Way** found itself spurned by most Black churches. This chapter will seek to explore this difficult chasm as well as prepare you for the following chapter on Black Power.

An Anthropologist's Spin On Black Pentecostalism and Black Power

The hot and public summer of 1967 brought different people for differing reasons to **The Way.** One who came introduced himself as an associate professor of anthropology from the University of Minnesota. Dr. Luther P. Gerlach was doing a study on movements of social transformation, and he wanted to include **The Way** in his work. His study sought to make the claim that there was a link between Black Pentecostalism and Black Power and that it was part of a cultural revolution that was "broader in scope than a mere social revolution in one society." Dr. Gerlach had already traveled to Port-au-Prince, Haiti, as well as Bogota, Colombia, and other places to do field work. He had come back to his own state to offer, at the safe distance of a sympathetic social scientist, a take on what was happening in the Twin Cities African-American community. 1967 was the "outbreak summer," as Gerlach tagged it, that witnessed a wave of protest to hit the streets not only in Minneapolis but in several cities throughout the United States.

Dr. Gerlach and his research team hung about **The Way** through the summer to return periodically the following year. History was in the making and so was his book. No doubt the professor was a sympathetic observer. He said as much as he admitted the sympathies of himself and his fellow researchers with the aims of Black Power.

Dr. Gerlach wryly captured in *People, Power, and Change: Movements of Social Transformation* the mood within the Black community with a telling difference that would separate people and groups out. He claimed Black conservatives viewed street violence as riots, Black militants saw them as revolutionary acts, while Black moderates saw the disturbances as signs of rebellion. The book sketched a political continuum of Black organizations as conservative, moderate, and militant.[1] Black groups are viewed in light of their response to public violence as exercised by Blacks. The more important question of how such groups view the exercise of power is only implied. Black churches, like conservative groups, had dissuaded themselves from overt use of power. Another way to say it was conservative groups worked within the system, moderates worked the system, and militants worked against it. It came down to how each group viewed power and its use.

Dr. Gerlach identifies the conservative wing with civil rights organizations, such as the national NAACP and Urban League that had been in existence for decades. Moderate groups were "community centers" that had emerged in more recent times that openly espoused Black Power. Minneapolis Citizen Community Center (CCC) was a moderate group that became more militant under new leadership that had earlier been organizers for the Poor People's March. The police riot reported in the previous chapter involved the leadership of the Minneapolis CCC.

On the other hand, **The Way** was "a new type of community center."[2] Dr. Gerlach comments on **The Way's** objective to "reach the unreachable"—the angry and alienated Black youth—simply confirmed the dominant view that urban riots where caused by such down-and-outers, as he termed them, and could be prevented if only this group could be reached. He called this the "deprivation causes riots" theory. The grand jury's public scold and criticism of **The Way** for contributing to the riot of 1967 by coddling the criminal element, whom obviously were to blame, certainly proved that such a theory was not only alive but working overtime in the minds of many people.

One feels in reading *People, Power, and Change: Movements of Social Transformation* that it is written for a White audience who want to know what is going on in a community they normally give no thought to. However, the book's declared intent is a study on movements of social transformation and to demonstrate the commonality Black Pentecostalism shared with Black Power. Dr. Gerlach saw similarities between them in type, if not in the content, of their ideologies.

He makes a startling suggestion that is worth the price of the book. It certainly surprised some academics, but it is hardly a surprise to anyone who worshipped in a Black church. "We will go even further and suggest ways in which Pentecostalism may be considered revolutionary, and Black Power religious."[3]

The book claims Pentecostalism is revolutionary because at its core is the radical conversion of the individual. The additional claim is Black Power movements are religious in asking for individual sacrifice for the greater good of justice. The professor rightly senses that behind all Black movements of reform and protest had been the Black church. What he does not fully draw out is the role that Black Folk Religion plays in creating a secular organization like **The Way**.

Professor Gerlach was right to recognize that the Troeltsch theory was inadequate to the study of Pentecostalism with its many vibrant hybrids. What was the Troeltsch theory? Ernest Troeltsch was a German philosopher of religion who, under the influence of Max Webber, the esteemed sociologist, came to see how religious thought played out in social reality.

Professor Troeltsch discusses this question in his book *The Social Teaching of the Christian Churches*[4] as he develops his basic sect-to-church typology. Simply stated, a religious group that begins as a sect, an independent group whose worship is simple, over time takes on the characteristics of a church not only in organization but also in liturgical forms of worship and dress. Troeltsch typology offers an approach in understanding the interaction of social history with religious groups. However, as typologies are not only illuminating, they are also limited.

In the American context, the sect-to-church typology took a twist as churches become more sectarian just as sects become more like churches. For instance, Episcopalians in America are known in Britain as Anglicans whose church is supported by the state. In America, no religious group is the state religion. So American Episcopalians, unlike the British Anglicans, raise their own funds like any free church in Britain, such as the British Methodists who are free of state support. Even so, Methodists in America today look nothing like their early frontier camp meetings. The early Methodist movement swept holiness across the American continent during the nineteenth century blown by the hot winds of evangelical fervor. Methodists of late have taken on the look of liturgy and dress of Episcopalians.

Even though Dr. Gerlach realizes the limitation of the sect-church typology, he never fully expands on the theory to aid his analysis of the underlying influences that mark the two-way relationship of Black Pentecostalism with Black Power. It is for this reason **The Way** is labeled a Black Power organization, yet by neglecting its roots in Black Folk Religion, Gerlach fails to point **The Way's** connection to the Black church. Oddly, the good doctor never mentions **The Way** by name in his book, as he never mentions the other ten organizations and groups he and his researches studied. His book, like the summer, began with promise, only to end with a sense of incompleteness.

A Well-Known Black Preacher's Spin On the Context of the Game

Reverend Albert B. Cleage Jr. came by **The Way** one day in 1967 to talk with Syl Davis and check out what he had heard as far east as Detroit where he served as pastor of the Shrine of the Black Madonna. He had no difficulty in understanding what **The Way** sought to accomplish. He immediately saw it as a part of a long struggle of Black Americans for human rights and human dignity.

I am in Syl Davis' office as Dr. Cleage comes in. He speaks to Syl, yet he is also speaking for my benefit, knowing I am a White clergyman. "White folks," he says adamantly, "need to hear the words of St. Paul. Get on your knees and repent. Black folks need to hear the Gospel. Stand up and march."

Dr. Cleage is a Christian minister seeking to weave Black Folk Religion to the on-going struggle of Black people. He advocates the rediscovery of the Black Messiah.[5] The Black Messiah is key to the recovery of Black people's true self-worth and dignity. He publicly declared, "We could not worship a Black Jesus until we had thrown off the shackles of self-hate." Reverend Cleage is one of the few Christian ministers of the day bold to say that the Black community cannot neglect its past and groups, like the Black Muslims, rejection of Christianity is a grave mistake.

Dr. Joseph Washington, an African-American academic, suggests in his book *Black Sects and Cults* that Reverend Cleage is a tragic figure.[6] Dr. Cleage's charismatic character loves controversy at the expense of detailed work demanded of community organization. The gift of right instincts and solid ideas is wasted in not seeing them through with a resolve that bears fruit in the Black community. In Dr. Washington's estimate, Dr. Cleage is not fulfilling the promise of Black Folk Religion.

The Way Recovers the Mandate of Black Folk Religion

In his book, Dr. Washington speaks of the various ways the Black church and Black sects fail to realize the mandate of Black Folk Religion. The Black church preaches a gospel appealing to middle class individuals. It gives hope to those who live in an unjust world of red line mortgages and job glass ceilings. Being loyal on the job, caring for the family, one will gain, for the upward mobile, a heavenly prize. However, in encouraging individual steadfastness, the Black church neglects the necessity for group action. In like fashion, Black sects offer protection for the lonely individual under the wings of God's angels that stay the evil grasp of Satan who wants to steal the soul before the tempting powers of discrimination and denigration. Both Black churches and Black sects fail to relate the gospel of Christ to the struggle for justice, the love of the cross to the exercise of power to gain justice.

Dr. Washington places the spin on Black Power and Black Pentecostalism, as understood both by Gerlach and Cleage, into a wider context. Black Pentecostalism is not revolutionary in the sense Dr. Gerlach speaks unless it addresses the necessary transformation of society in which the transformed individual lives. Dr. Cleage may preach a revolutionary Black Power gospel, but it is only rhetoric if it does not issue in action models of power that affect social change. Oddly, both Dr. Gerlach and Dr. Cleage reveal how Black Pentecostalism has lost its moorings in Black culture. Dr. Washington strongly suggests that Black churches and Black sects are ill conceived when they divert the longing of Black people away from the struggle of justice. Black culture is a way of life searching for healthiness of soul and community that can only be enfranchised by the exercise of power. Whenever Black culture is denied in its quest for justice, it returns to its cultic roots to emerge openly to address the need for communal health, a need met only by the address and exercise of power.

The Way was not doctrinally Christian, yet its espousal of Black Power was rooted in Black Folk Religion. **The Way** was a movement that revealed neither bitterness nor fear, but a mental resolve and social aspiration that is at the soul of African-American people. **The Way**, like groups before it, sought economic and social power not for itself, nor only for African-American people, but for all those who were impoverished and oppressed.

Syl Davis was chosen by circumstance in being in the right place at the right time; more, he was the right man for the right social movement for change, who like those who had gone on before him was both a visionary and a dreamer with a practical touch. One of the last things Syl wrote was a speech that reiterated the claim that **The Way's** very existence was a call to power. This is what he wrote. "Freedom, as the absence of all restraint, and power, the ability to negotiate on equal terms in the larger community, have their source in the power of God." These thoughts were in his prepared message to the Seventeenth Annual Meeting of the board of directors. It was a meeting never held at **The Way's** new building as it was closed along with its program in late 1984. Though Syl's words were never given, these words are still alive and need to be heard for such thoughts express the original vision that brought **The Way** into existence.

The Way's self-direction for our community is needed now more than ever. Our participation in the institution of the larger society must come home. Those of us involved in the struggle must be inspired with the faith and hope of our founders. This is the challenge of **The Way** as it begins the new era of our future. We must maintain clarity of purpose and goals, for we must be unceasing in our effort to increase the consciousness of our community in which we live. **The Way** is for ALL PEOPLE and that responsibility for our survival must now be assumed by those of us who benefited from our earlier struggle. As long as some of us remain in the bondage of poverty, then all of us as people are in bondage. "Inasmuch as you have done it to one of the least of my brethren, you have done it to me."[7] It is a merciless description of our responsibility for one another.[8]

That is the mandate of Black Folk Religion. It is a faith well acquainted with a deeper mercy that lies beneath the never tiring call to renew the struggle for justice. It finds its abode in the human yearning for freedom that cannot be turned back ever since that first cry of slaves in an Egyptian brickyard. In 1966 it summoned people, Black and White, poor and rich, to a place on Plymouth Avenue in a midwestern city. Compelled by a common hope and earnest desire, they worked and scrapped together to bring a small measure of justice to a world that has long denied its coming. **The Way** was born to keep alive the dream that boldly believes until all people are free no one is truly free.

The Way and Black Power

The Long Hot Summer of 1966:
The Way and the Definition Game

Anticipation mixed with foreboding was keenly felt across this nation during the summer of 1966. "The long hot summer" was media's way of describing the growing unrest in African-American communities coupled with an increased anxiety in neighboring White conclaves. It was the summer Black Power's nomenclature eclipsed the rhetoric of Civil Rights. That summer was the midwife to the birth of **The Way**.

Mahmoud El-Kati walked into **The Way** one day in the fall of 1966. He asked Syl Davis, the director, if he could teach a course on Black history. A recent graduate from Wilberforce University in Cleveland, Ohio, Mahmoud was eager to teach. He was ready to share his knowledge of Black history with anyone who would listen. In 1966 there were no Black Studies programs in the Twin Cities. Syl listened and when he heard the passion in this young man and his willingness to teach for little or nothing, he hired Milt Williams, as he was known in those days, on the spot.

Mahmoud El-Kati brought an understanding of the African-American struggle for freedom along with the play of power in an ongoing definition game of who is defining whom and for what reason and to what effect. Mahmoud revealed what the high stakes around the struggle were about in an article he wrote for **The Way** newsletter entitled, "The Definition Game."

> You see, one defines to contain and to categorize, and that is the meaning of definitions in any struggle...Albert Camus, the French philosopher, said that a slave begins to exist as a free man—when he says no! I believe this; the first need of a free people is to be able to define themselves and state their terms and make their oppressors recognize them. The first thing that the oppressor must lose is the power of definition over the oppressed...and until a wretched and disinherited people learn to cope with and win the psychological game of definition, they will forever remain slaves.[1]

The definition game had begun in earnest and **The Way** became a controversial lightning rod with the powers to be over whose definition would win the day.

Violence: Depends on Who is Doing It to Whom

Smoke rose on the Minneapolis horizon that summer of 1966 to cause a great stir. When Black people went on the rampage on Plymouth Avenue the White community couldn't understand it. The use of violence was wrong, they said. What had been forgotten and left out of history books but seared into the memory of African-Americans was the race riots in East St. Louis, July 1917, and in Tulsa, Oklahoma, 1921.[2] In the summer of 1919 alone there were over twenty major race riots. During this period "race riot" meant White Americans murdering, pillaging, and plundering in Black communities.

Racial violence stalked much closer to home. There was the near riot of several thousand White citizens in 1931 that gathered outside the home of a Black man who had bought a house in an all-White neighborhood in Minneapolis. White people sought to buy the house back, but he refused to sell. Then young people started throwing garbage and refuse against his home as the *Minneapolis Tribune* ran headlines that acted like incendiaries that July. The headlines read "Home Stoned in Race Row" with subtitles, as they did in those days, that read "Sale of House to Negro Stirs Neighborhood" and "Several Hundred Gather on the Avenue to Hurl Missiles" and again "Gun Squads Called to Disperse Crowd."

Those headlines brought more people out to see what was happening. Soon threatening crowds of over a thousand surrounded the house. One night the police got the man and his family out safely by police squad car. Other times, a few friends along with a detachment of police, came to keep watch through the night. The Black owner declared boldly, "I have a right to stay in the neighborhood in light of the democratic principles of this government! Nobody asked me to move out when I was in France fighting in mud and water for this country." The White mayor surprised people by supporting the man's right to live where he chose and stationed police outside his home to protect him and his family. Hot tempers began to flare. One of the vocal voices in the crowd was heard to say, "You all know me; if there is going to be any burning, I am going to be in on it; if there is going to be any stringing up, I am going to be in on it; but I think we had better let the police manage it."[3]

In 1920, mob lynching tragically took the lives of three men in Duluth. A crowd of White men broke into the jail and hung three Black men who were working for a traveling carnival because they had been accused of molesting a White woman. That mob lynching prompted the Minnesota State Legislature in 1921 to pass an Anti-Lynching Law. H. Rap Brown had gotten it right. Violence was as American as apple pie.

This is a history White Americans had forgotten or chose to forget. At **The Way** Mahmoud El-Kati put such violence into historical perspective.

> **Violence:** If you examine history very carefully, you will find that violence in America is almost immune from censorship, unless it is prefaced by the term Negro! I am opposed to violence, not just Negro violence. Innocent little Black

girls being blown to death on highways is violent; lynching is violent; castration is violent. The beatings endured by SNCC [Student Nonviolent Coordinating Committee] workers during the Civil Rights era was violent. Men who sit in Congress and use the law as an instrument for oppression of Black people are violent men. Racial discrimination itself does untold psychological violence to the human personality. We live in a nation born in violence. Violence, it seems to me, is the religion of this nation (that which we owe our highest respect). The Negro was born in violence because slavery was a violent institution.[4]

The battle over the definition game was heating up as it was getting down and heavy.

1966: Times are a 'Changin'

What is Going On

—Marvin Gaye[5]

What was going on in the United States in 1966? Internationally, the United States was sinking its military boots deeper into the mire of an undeclared war in Vietnam, a place many Americans couldn't find on a map. Before the end of the decade Americans knew where Vietnam was and that the war could never be won. Within two years, both Dr. Martin Luther King, Jr. and Senator Robert Kennedy, who both spoke out against racism and the war, were slain.

In 1966, Reverend Dr. Martin Luther King, Jr. accepted the position of co-chair for Clergy-Laity Against the War. In a rally in Washington D.C., King set forth his convictions. He believed the war against the peasants in Vietnam was akin to the war against Black people in America. He declared the war in Vietnam was taking necessary resources away from the War on Poverty in the United States. He spoke of the high proportion of Black young men who were dying in Vietnam compared to Whites. Blacks and Whites can die on the same battlefield, Dr. King noted, yet back home they cannot attend the same schools. To see the poor in Vietnam, their villages being burned, was another form of brutal cruelty against the poor. King said angry young men in the ghettos in the North had taught him something valuable. When he told them they could not solve their problems with Molotov cocktails and rifles but only through nonviolent action, they quickly came back to tell him to quit preaching nonviolence with all the violence going on in Vietnam. Dr. King said it was then he knew he could not raise his voice against the violence of the oppressed in the ghettos without speaking out against the United States government who was acting as the greatest purveyor of violence in the world.[6]

This message proved to be provocative and frightening to the White establishment. Dr. King was already under surveillance by J. Edgar Hoover's FBI as King's private conversations were being taped. The noose was being tied.

Cry of Black Power on a Civil Rights March

In 1966 James Meredith, who had been the first Black student at Ole Miss (University of Mississippi), was shot in a march he was leading in Greenwood, Mississippi. On the protest march that followed, Stokley Carmichael made his famous Black Power speech. Mr. Carmichael was a firebrand who stoked the burning embers of discontent smoldering in the heated grates of several major cities throughout America that turbulent summer. Stokley Carmichael caught the itchy ears of young Blacks that were disenchanted with Black nonviolence as it did not stop the violence against Black people. On the James Meredith march from Memphis to Jackson, Mississippi, the young changed the anthem of nonviolence "We Shall Overcome" to "We Shall Overrun." Stokley Carmichael knew his Black Power speech would set a new agenda for Black America even at the risk of offending Dr. King who was taken by surprise.[7]

Stokley Carmichael had grown up in Trinidad before moving on to the Bronx and attending Howard University. At Howard, he began work with the Student Nonviolent Coordinating Committee [SNCC] and, after graduation, worked with SNCC organizing in Black communities north and south as he rose in the ranks to chair SNCC by the summer of 1966. A year later, he published the provocative book *Black Power* he co-authored with Charles V. Hamilton, a professor and chairman of the Department of Political Science at Roosevelt University in Chicago. Stokley Carmichael represented a new voice, a voice that demanded to be heard. Taylor Branch, who has written on the Civil Rights Movement, offers several instances where Mr. Carmichael had chafed under the yoke of nonviolence and questioned it as a strategy.[8]

Mr. Carmichael and Dr. Hamilton viewed the struggle and the use of power far differently from Dr. King. Their perspective was political; whereas, King always understood the struggle as being religious and moral. Dr. King later wrote his critique of Black Power in his final book, *Where Do We Go From Here?* However, by that time King's voice was nearly lost beneath the alarm and clamor that began in the summer of 1966. The White backlash and the escalation of violence, Dr. King feared, would nearly remove the Civil Right Movement from the mind of most White Americans who associated Black Power with violence. White liberals called upon old line Negro leadership to denounce Black Power. Dr. King took an advertisement out in the *New York Times*. The man who was against the use of slogans had found himself using them. The caption read "It Is Not Enough To Condemn Black Power."[9] It was clear the power play behind the definition game was changing.

Black Power Moves to the Front Page

The book *Black Power* issued a call to Black people to rise up in a display of unity and power against the White establishment. It put on the front page the change in society that was coming down. Like a Pentecostal preacher, the rhetoric struck fire in the heart of the dispossessed and quickened the dead as the authors laid down the terms that marked the new phase of the struggle. The call to Black Power, meant it was time for self-definition. *Black Power* stated the new agenda to the growing resentment to the word Negro. It was a necessity for Black people to get rid of the label Negro for it was a White man's term. The Civil Rights Movement with its integration-ist agenda would be opposed. It was a Negro delusion to continue to believe that a way to improve one's lot in life was to be integrated into White society when integration was fearfully defined by White Americans as race-mixing.

Mahmoud El-Kati, **The Way's** Education Director, with wry humor and candor put it succinctly: "The Black leaders would say, we want to integrate; the Whites would say no, you want to marry my daughter. And these Black leaders would say no, I don't want to marry your daughter, we just want to be your brother; we don't want to be your brother-in-law."[10] The new note that was being heard was the rejection of the middle class value of assimilation for it represented too high a price to pay in having Black people hand over their history and unique identity in order to join a class that perpetuated racism.

The call in 1966 to Black Power marked the growing divide between the Black community's sense of justice as opposed to mid-dle class morality. Each is different in its thinking. The middle class regarded itself as individuals. Black Power was a way for Black people to act in concert, exhibit their solidarity in the fight for justice and equality. Mahmoud El-Kati wrote these challenging words to the middle class Negro in those hours.

I believe I have some understanding and appreciation of the very special and delicate plight of the middle class Negro that man or woman who, as an individual, has encountered and overcome the tremendous odds stacked against him by the hypocrisy of American democracy. The middle class Negro has taken the personal creed of James Weldon Johnson and used it as a guiding light, a pillow of strength in a hostile world. "I will not let one prejudice person, or one million, or one hundred million to blight my life. I will not allow preju-dice or any of its attendant humiliations or injustices bear me down to spiritual defeat. My inner life is my own, and I shall defend and maintain its integrity against all the powers of hell."

The middle class Negro is the only member of American society who has literally practiced rugged individualism, for he was, and still for the most part, is the only individual of a major ethnic group who has thrived without the basis of power, solidarity, or support from his group, with few exceptions. He has accepted, and still accepts, the values, mores, moral hang-ups, and general lifestyle of White America without questioning the inconsistency and duplicity of them. The middle class Negro has historically been a conformist and, in many cases, an ever conformist. Lambasted and put down by many people because of his unabashed desire for acceptance by those who deny his existence, the Black Anglo Saxon or Black Bourgeois, as he has oft times been scornfully called, has found himself caught between two hostile worlds—one Black, one White. He rejects one world; the other rejects him. At a given time he is; at another time he is not. On the one hand he can, and on the other hand, he cannot. A man in limbo.[11]

Definition Game Turns Vicious: False Charge of Reverse Racism

The rhetoric turned hot when the White backlash began labeling Black Power advocates as "Black racists." Mr. Carmichael and Dr. Hamilton denied any such identification. Their point was that racism perpetuates itself only through instruments of institutional power. Power would only yield to power. The goal of Black self-determination was to exercise power in society's decision-making processes that influenced Black people.

Influential Black churchmen put an ad in the *New York Times* so they could be heard above the countercharges of Black racism. The preachers made it clear the real problem was the failure of American leadership to use power to create equal opportunity in life as well as law, not the anguished cry for Black power.[12]

The Way Practices What it Preaches

The authors of *Black Power* issued a call for Black people to close ranks claiming that Black people work together and do things for themselves. **The Way** logo [that appears through the book as the mast head on chapter divisions]—upside down me is we—embodied the philosophy and practice of solidarity articulated by Syl Davis, "we can do what I can't." Working together for themselves was turning things upside down. The poor and people of color had to stop thinking of themselves as isolated and powerless individuals and begin acting together as a group. **The Way** did not represent people of color and the poor but rather worked with them so they could act in concert on their own behalf. Syl Davis put it in equalitarian terms in an article he wrote for **The Way** newsletter entitled, "What Is The Way?"

> **The Way** represents a voice—hope for the people who before had little or no hope. Through **The Way** the people are being heard. Our hope is becoming a reality. **The Way** has made a commitment to all people; that commitment is that we respect each individual as he or she is. Every person who enters our door enters for a reason. A need, either to give or receive. Hopefully, both.
>
> In order for us to continue our growth, we need YOUR ideas, YOUR hopes, YOUR desires to our total community. We do not establish programs except at the request of a person, or a group of people. It is not the way of **The Way** to set up a program and then sit back and wonder why it fails. We do not do things for people, but rather with them. We build on their very strengths and their successes. It is not our intent to walk behind pushing, or ahead pulling; we do, however, walk together progressing.
>
> **The Way** is more than just a youth center or a community center or a cultural center. **The Way** is a way of life.[13]

The Way followed the admonition of Frederick Douglas, the nineteenth century African-American apologist for equality and freedom, regarding the use of power. Douglas prophetic voice spoke a greater truth than the nation could bare and yet could not evade when the Civil War came nine years later. It is an abiding truth and one that this nation cannot escape: the American people would never be free until all its people were free and equal. That would only come with struggle. It was the struggle that was shaping America in 1852 when Douglas wrote these fiery words, words that still shape the struggle for freedom.

> Power concedes nothing without a demand. It never did and it never will. . . . Men may not get all they pay for in this world, but they must certainly pay for all they get. If we ever get free from the oppressions and wrongs heaped upon us, we must pay for their removal. We must do this by labor, by suffering, by sacrifice, and if needs be, by our lives and the lives of others.[14]

The definition game was more than a game. It was a question of right and wrong. 1966 was not a time to sit on the fence. And when it came to **The Way**, no one sat on the fence for long.

FIVE

THE WAY
STRUGGLE GOES ON:

Creating the [Neighbor]hood

The biblical book of Deuteronomy is Israel's neighbor book
outlining a revolutionary social vision.
Moses come down from Sinai,
remembering the first three commandments says:
"For the Lord your God is God of gods
and Lord of lords, the great God, mighty and awesome..."
(Deuteronomy 10:17a)
then Moses remembers the next seven commandments.
He takes up a new note as he speaks about the neighborhood:
"...who is not partial and takes no bribe
who executes justice for the orphan and the widow,
and who loves the stranger, providing them food and clothing."
(Deuteronomy 10:17b-18)
Then comes the mandate to create God's neighborhood:
"You shall also love the stranger,
for you were strangers in the land of Egypt."
(Deuteronomy 10:19)

—Walter Brueggemann[1]

The Way Toward Inclusive Education

Antioch-Minneapolis Communivesity

We reversed the academic process.
We take what a person has already done
and try put it into a theoretical framework
through the course of events here at the communiversity
where one takes the time to unbias his thoughts.

—Gwyn Jones-Davis-Pyle[1]

Antioch-Minneapolis Communiversity: Early Seedlings Bear Fruit

Antioch-Minneapolis Communiversity [A-MC] was a unique experiment in higher education during the 1970s. It offered a college education to persons that otherwise would not have gone to college. Education, at its best, teaches people how to think for themselves, helps persons to develop the faculty for critical thought so they can evaluate for themselves the significance of their own life experiences and act upon them. Such was **A-MC's** high promise, a promise that had its start at **The Way** years before.

Shape of Education at The Way

The Way had worked from the very beginning to reformulate educational programs that made sense to people of color. Mahmoud

El-Kati articulated the reasons why formal education failed so many people. In doing so, he began to set down the basic understanding of **The Way's** approach to education.

> The word education can be defined as the process of training and developing knowledge, skill, the mind, and character. In our modern fast changing society, it is crystal clear, despite the abundance of formal education institutions, that the process of formal education does not adequately meet the needs of a substantial segment of the American population—particularly, minority background peoples. It is because of this void that this effort is being made.
>
> By offering a comprehensive, creative, non-institutional educational program at **The Way**, three specific aims are in mind: to combat some of the negative environmental forces which contribute to poor interest and performance of the in-school child of the community; to promote a creative learning situation for the out of school in the community and give positive direction to his life; and to stimulate interest among all adult age groups in playing a more active role in uplifting the well being of the total community in social, civic, and cultural life.[2]

The focus of education was in three areas: heritage, culture, and leadership development. A brief description from each of these areas of concentration reveals the intent and purpose of the course instruction.

> **Heritage:** An important psychological need of any people is that of heritage, of having a sense of history, and an ethnic identity. At **The Way**, we have found that there is a dearth of the most fundamental knowledge and appreciation of heritage or tradition as it relates to the largest social and/or ethnic group of the community being served by **The Way**. To meet this vital social and psychological need, a course in the study of the Afro-American in American life is being offered.

Culture: The cultural complex of our community, city, and state has become immensely difficult for many disadvantaged people to keep pace with because of the far reaching changes of recent years. Rapid change has had an immeasurable impact on the community that is being served by **The Way**. Social disorganization in family life, transience, and educational deficiencies are the negative factors, which contribute to the underdeveloped cultural orientation of the community. The cultural orientation studies at **The Way** is designed to diminish the cultural lag that exists within the community.

Leadership Development: The need for well organized social living within the community coincides with the shortage of good community leaders. Scarce commodity of leadership is present and latent in the community, but it is largely uninformed, uninspired, and underdeveloped. The leadership development program at **The Way** is geared to tap people of all ages in the community who show some leadership potential.[3]

Racism as a Mental Illness: The Tillman Influence

James and Mary Tillman offered a course on racism as early as 1963. James Tillman was at the time director of the Minnesota Council of Churches Fair Housing program, a position he held from 1959 to 1965. The Kerner Report had yet to be published.[4] Its publication was the first public acknowledgement by an agency of the government that the riots in American cities during the sixties were caused by White racism. The Tillmans believed the report gave a correct diagnosis of a national illness but failed to offer a cure. In response, they wrote "A Layman's Guide for Detecting and Treating Racism." The pamphlet made the case that racism is a mental illness endemic to White persons. Racism is a sickness that goes undetected as it is practiced collectively making a mental illness normative and accepted behavior. This was the foundational insight for the Tillman course on racism.

The Tillman course exposed racism by having seminar White participants confront their own prejudices and then relearn new attitudes and behavior. The Tillman treatment that offered vinegar instead of sugar in detecting and treating racism was outlined in their pamphlet "What Is Your Racism Quotient?"[5] Jim and Mary Tillman believed their seminar offered a prescription toward a cure of the mental sickness of racism. A person's recovery toward health was measured by a change in life perspective toward people of color. This change evidenced itself further in the work for social justice based on the equality of power for both Black and White groups.

Gwyn Jones-Davis' program D.A.R.E. [Development of the Abilities of Rejected Egos], developed for **The Way** in 1967, was largely dependent on the Tillman's definition of racism as a mental illness. The program worked with African-American young people labeled "behavior malcontents." D.A.R.E. sought to empower young people of color to discover their true worth by seeing that they were not the source of the problem but evidence of a sick system that systematically abused the self-identity and esteem of young African-American persons.

The Way's educational focus was primarily cleansing the ill effects of racism particularly on African-American young people and adults. It did not see as its mission the necessity of offering racism courses for the White community. However, things changed by late 1969 as the **University of The Way** offered its first racism course for White participants.

Within two years the **Antioch-Minneapolis Communiversity [A-MC]**, an outgrowth of the **University of The Way**, began teaching a course on racism, required of public school teachers. To Tillmans' insight that racism was a mental sickness was added the insight of Franz Fanon, thus seeing racism as a mental illness within a social context. Fanon demonstrated how racism worked as a mechanism of submission creating the need for the other both in the master and the slave personalities. [The racist need for the other is a dynamic of mental illness explored in the chapter "The Way and Ishmael."] The **A-MC** course exposed the workings of racism in the dominant mind-set in its need for the other. Projecting its own mental illness racism disfigures the figure of the other, yet it is its own image, hidden to oneself. Oscar Wilde's handsome Dorian Gray, whose portrait captures his hidden self, while he remains before the world youthful and unblemished. Yet sickness finally breaks out with Dorian Gray's destruction of the portrait. Racism's claim can be broken once one is made conscious of the workings of racism. As one moves toward new perspectives of health so one becomes engaged in the equal power sharing with persons of color in fighting for social change that begins dismantling the horrid portraits of racism.

A New Model for Higher Education

John Dewey, the American philosopher and exponent of education, offers the insight that freedom of the mind, the freedom to make one's own judgments based on observation and intelligence, was the counterweight to social control.[6] The **University of The Way** sought to promote the conscious use of intelligence and observation in the exercise of freedom from social control. It carried on the early education efforts at **The Way** that taught grade and high school students labeled unreachable. The university would be one of the first in the Twin Cities to teach college level courses in the African-American community. This idea of the university began in 1968 through **The Way's** association with Augsburg College in Minneapolis. The statement of purpose for the **University of The Way** reveals the thinking at the time among persons connected to **The Way's** expanding education program.

> The **University of The Way** is founded upon the proposition that the essence of a democracy is the right of every member to be himself, and that one of the best measures of the strength of any democracy is the diversity of its membership. The **University of The Way** was established because of the existing systems of education in America has failed to acknowledge and to comprehend the unique history, culture, and personality of all American ethnic communities. In ignoring the condition of these Americans, the present system of education has failed to understand the American condition as a whole. America's self-knowledge is only as great as her understand-

ing of the experience of all its members. This has not been the case in the past except to relate to ethnic communities of color with intolerance and brutality. The **University of The Way**, however, questions far more than the historical perspective of the existing educational system. It questions the honesty and existence of a society which denies the right and the humanity of all but one ethno-cultural group that makes it up.[7]

The initial plan for The **University of The Way** was to bring persons of different cultures and backgrounds together in a uncommon learning environment. The college student, usually middle class, took credited courses in an inner city setting with students who came from the inner city. Eventually, the students from the inner city would go on to take courses on a college campus. The **University of The Way** faculty included African-American and Native-American teachers, as well as European-Americans who offered courses on cultural perspectives unique to their culture. Courses included the challenge of intra-cultural communication along with an analysis of social institutions and society from the perspectives of people of color.

This pioneering effort can be largely lost on us if we do not know there were a small number of persons of color attending Minnesota colleges in the late sixties. It must be remembered that was a time when few, if any, of Minnesota's schools of higher learning offered courses in Black Studies.

In 1970, Antioch College made overtures to the university to become one of their branch schools. By 1971, the **University of The Way** became a member of a consortium of colleges with a new name. The first part of the name **Antioch-Minneapolis** signified a new contractual relationship with a college that had a national reputation. **A-MC**, as it was called, became part of a bold experiment of higher education offering a four-year Bachelor of Arts degree. With its network of schools, Antioch College in Yellow Springs, Ohio, reached out to a multicultural population that was growing throughout the United States.

Antioch College was an outgrowth, in the early nineteenth century, of the struggle for freedom and equality. Schools of higher learning were planted in the non-slave territories by the abolitionists along with an assembly of religious groups that included the Baptists, Methodists, Presbyterians, and later, the Unitarians. By 1850, a plan was approved for the construction of a college in the Ohio Valley that would be somewhat radical for its time—co-educational and non-sectarian. The college would boldly take to its name Antioch, the place where the followers of Christ were first called, in derision, Christians. The college's first president was the noted philosopher, educator, and statesman Horace Mann. Antioch would go on to establish a reputation for experimental education during the thirties as it offered college credit for life experience learning. By the sixties Antioch was broadening that vision by offering alternative learning strategies in various settings throughout the United States.

The second part of the name **Communiversity** spoke of the school's unique approach to education by bringing the university into the community as it gave access to a college education to a new population. With a sudden increase in enrollment, **A-MC** moved to a larger building at 1708 Oak Park on the Near North Side, a few blocks away from **The Way**.

A-MC offered a unique style of learning to help persons analyze and solve their own problems. Problem solving education places emphasis on intentionality. It epitomizes the character of consciousness, being aware of one's own decision making and its impact on others. It is an authentic vocation when one engages in inquiry and creative transformation. **A-MC** approach to education prized cognition in its ability to bring the critique of one's own creative intelligence, coupled with keen observation, to bear on the development of one's life strategies. The communiversity supplied the tools of conventional wisdom, often in unconventional ways, so that students could complete their tasks.

Formation as the Key to Educational Reform: The Journey

Pedagogy of the Oppressed was a well used text at **A-MC**.[8] Its author, Paulo Freire, had learned, living under Brazil's oppressive regime, the high stake of becoming free in mind and spirit. He had understood that education became oppressive when it sought to have persons adapt to their situation, not change it. Dr. Freire espousal of education developed a practical plan of action and reflection sought to transform social structures so people could be free to be themselves.

The Journey was the beginning course required of students entering **Antioch-Minneapolis Communiversity**. The course not only introduced the student to the curriculum but also to its methodology. **A-MC's** methodology was radical—seeking to get to the root of what we know and why we know what we know and how we can know differently.

The opening dialogue asked the question "What makes the Emerald City green in the book *Wizard of Oz?*" If one never read the book but had seen the Judy Garland film than the trick happened before one's eyes. The trick was technicolor. The movie's opening scenes, filmed in black and white, were filled with dust bowl images known to most Americans in 1939 when the movie was first shown. After a tornado lifted Judy and her dog, Toto, out of this world to land among the Munchkins, the scene changed. The audience had landed, along with Judy and Toto, in Hollywood and in the twinkling of an eye, the scene was transformed into technicolor. Technicolor was to the movie what green glasses were in the book, the ticket to get into the Emerald City. The use of technicolor was more a slight of hand than glasses, yet both were the work of a wizard, who knew more than one world, enabling this trickster to change the ordinary world to make it look like the Emerald City.

The lecture went on to claim that everyone wears some form of green glasses that we called a mind-set. Each person views the world through a cultural lens that is the work of the wizards of acculturation. And every society works through the invisible lens of a dominate mind-set.[9] Everyone on the planet lives out of the power of images that pictures life for one. We cannot live in a world without having a mind-set and certainly we cannot live fully with it. A mind-set is dynamic, ever changing, so one can learn how to change the images that determine behavior, values, even our very thought patterns.

Epistemology deals with that part of philosophy concerned with the origin, nature, and limit of knowledge. The radical epistemological efforts of the faculty, though differing in style, shared one common criteria; namely, seeking what Paulo Freire called the "indispensable condition" that brought humanity closer to its destiny. Human beings are driven by their nature to act, and also compelled by their nature as free spirits to relate their action to a total scheme of meaning. Furthermore persons are prompted in their freedom of mind to seek an ultimate source of meaning. Such was the underlying passion that moved the faculty as it sought to discover what is true and what is false in the conflicting claims of competing schools of thought, as viewed from beyond the dominant mind-set. So equipped, students developed their own life philosophy to engage the world of their reentry where ever freedom was denied or delayed. Such was the motive power behind the formational thrust of **Antioch-Minneapolis Communiversity.**

A-MC Became Unfocused

The **Antioch-Minneapolis Communiversity** offered a core curriculum in four areas: Law and Justice, Humanities, Cultural Studies, Social Sciences. Law and Justice became the major for most students. **A-MC** graduates included federal marshals, a warden of a major prison, probation officers, several students became lawyers and specialists in legal research, a few became advocates in Hennepin county probation department. One student, some thought to be funny, went on to become a well-known comic by the name of Louie Anderson.

By 1972, **A-MC** expanded its program to include "College Behind Walls." It provided college courses for the incarcerated at three correctional institutions: St. Cloud Reformatory for young men, Shakopee maximum security prison for women, and Stillwater maximum security prison for men. Financial assistance for students was made available through various financial aid sources that included National Direct Student Loan, Educational Opportunity Grant, Antioch-Minneapolis Tuition Grant, along with Law Enforcement Education Program. Student loans were guaranteed by Antioch College in Yellow

Springs. The fact that many of these loans to prisoners were never fully repaid jeopardized the **A-MC's** relation with Antioch College.

During this time the **A-MC** board authorized the purchase of a mansion on Mount Curve near the Guthrie Theater in Minneapolis. The mansion was bought at a price of several hundred thousand dollars for **A-MC's** president, Gwyn Jones-Davis-Pyle, and her husband, Jerry Pyle, the school's finance director. The growing debt in the payment of student loans coupled with the purchase of expensive property viewed to be beyond the means of the school would soon bring a crisis of confidence. Antioch of Yellow Springs, after lengthy negotiations with **A-MC**, decided its best course was to pay the loans at a great cost to itself and in so doing decided to cut its relationship with **A-MC**, prompting the school to close in 1979.

The Seed that Became a Learning Tree

What must not be forgotten is the pioneering work **Antioch-Minneapolis Communiversity** accomplished in developing learning strategies to reach marginalized persons, as well as bringing various persons together in intercultural learning situations that has borne fruit in other places in the Twin Cities. Metropolitan State College is one school of higher education that has gone on to develop **A-MC's** work in life experience learning. Mahmoud El-Kati, former faculty member at **A-MC** and now retired from the faculty at Macalester College, continues to teach new generations with words that have the passion and fire of Frederick Douglass: "Let me give you a word of the philosophy of reform. The history of the progress of human liberty shows that all concessions made to her august claims have been born of earnest struggle. If there is no struggle. . . ."[10]

As stated at the outset, education at its best teaches people how to think for themselves, to develop the faculty for critical thought so they can evaluate the significance of their own life experiences and then act so as to transform their world. **Antioch-Minneapolis Communiversity** offered that high promise that benefited many, a promise first articulated by those early storytellers and dreamers and teachers at **The Way**.

The Way Toward Restorative Justice

Prison Rehabilitation Brought Home

The spirit of liberty is the spirit that is not sure it is right;
the spirit of liberty is the spirit that seeks to understand the merits
of other men and women;
the spirit of liberty is the spirit that weighs their interests alongside
its own without bias;
the spirit of liberty remembers that not even a sparrow falls to earth unheeded.
The spirit of liberty is the spirit of him who,
nearly two thousand years ago,
taught man that lesson it has never learned,
but has never quite forgotten,
that there may be a kingdom where the least shall be heard
and considered side by side with the greatest.

—Judge Learned Hand[1]

Minnesota Nice Ain't So Nice: Minnesota Leads the Nation in Imprisonment Ratio

Minnesotans, who like to think of themselves as being nice and civil, woke on an early sunny June day to the uncivil and alarming news that their state had the worst record of all fifty states in racial disparity of those who end up in prison. People were shocked by the news, contained in a study by Human Rights Watch, a New York based research and advocacy group, that a Black man's chances of going to prison in Minnesota were twenty-seven times greater than a White man who had committed the same crime.[2]

The *Star Tribune* article did not use the qualifying words, "arrested and jailed" because a great deal of white-collar crime does not show up on crime statistics, a claim made by Edwin H. Southerland in the *American Sociological Review* written over sixty years ago.[3] Such is the different fates between the uncommon and the common criminal.

The ruling elite of the corporate community has the power to keep their names off the books and so their criminal activity will not become a criminal record. Friedrick von Schiller, the German philosopher, put the terms of power politics in this light, "It is criminal to steal a purse, daring to steal a fortune, a mark of greatness to steal a crown. The blame diminishes as the guilt increases."[4]

State Leaders Urge Deeper Look at Causes

"It's going to take some time and research and self-examination by all participants in the criminal justice system to understand the issue and how we can make some changes."[5] Such was State Corrections Commissioner Sheryl Ramstad Hvass innocuous response to the Human Watch Report. The commissioner was once a municipal judge whom Ron Edwards, a Black activist and resident of the North Side, accused of foul play in the whiping away of his trial transcripts. Edward's exposé is told in his book *The Minneapolis Story: Through My Eyes.*[6]

We do not have to look far nor take much time to understand what has been said time and again. Cornel West, professor of African-American Studies and of the Philosophy of Religion at Princeton, one of the foremost persons studying African-American young people, makes it clear that a major factor for crime in the Black community is the nihilistic cultural mindset that pervades the thinking of African-American teenagers. Nihilism comes down to being nobody, nil, no count with nothing to do, being nothing with nowhere to go. The consumer society via television comes into folks' homes hour upon hour, every day, every week of every month of every year one grows up, pushing products, convincing one that in order to be worthy one must have sexually attractive things: clothes; cars; TV; cell phones; Nikes; you name it, you can have it. Of course, you got to have the means to do that. When you do not have the means—no bread, no money, no power—you use the necessary means, even if it is mean, to get what you want. The brother on the corner is yet another capitalist entrepreneur doing his thing. His illegal means is more out-front, more visible than what happens in corporate boardrooms where often illegal maneuvering goes on at a much higher power pitch. What society can't admit out loud, our movies show. People watch film after film about gangsters on the street and in the corporate world, all engaged in one great struggle, the struggle of the fittest to survive.[7]

Robert Merton, a American social theorist, wrote over thirty years ago in his famous essay "Social Structure and Anomie" that society imbues its young with strong goals with one hand and then takes it away with the other by denying some of its people any socially legitimate means for reaching these goals. According to Cornel West, male African-American teenagers enmeshed in poverty are prime examples of Merton's theory.

Battle in the Classroom: Violence Imbued in an Idealistic Philosophy

The public schools have as their mission in a democracy to rescue children from the society's limitations of racism, class, and family situations by offering them access to a world where they may expand their imagination and live out their strong ambitions. Educators, particularly in inner city schools, often seek to deflect the social apartheid that encumbers the poor and minorities of color by offering an idealistic philosophy that could be characterized by Abraham Maslow's self-actualizing human being. When such a philosophy is espoused, then educators unwittingly play into a false ideology that convinces school children they are all bright, capable, and can beat the odds by becoming someone important in the world. Such idealistic theories are fine motivational speeches to up-and-coming middle class youth, but seldom play out in life for inner city young people.

The Minneapolis schools' "beat the odds" is a case of an idealistic theory gone awry. Mr. Edwards offers a devastating critique of such an approach. The metaphor, he says, shows that the schools are playing with children's lives as if they were dice. People know that in every game of chance some win and many lose. Schools are not casinos where playing craps turns up crap. It is child abuse, Mr. Edwards claims, when many students are unable to read and write and do numbers. The school district slogan "beat the odds" doesn't tell us what the odds really are. As recently as 2001, only 17 percent of Black male students graduated from Minneapolis high schools.[8]

Ron Edwards offers the assessment that The National Assessment of Education Progress reported in June 2001 that "a third of America's fourth graders are illiterate." Mr. Edwards goes on to point out the subtle use of statistics published to a public that does not have the complete story. The fine print of the report reveals that for Hispanic fourth graders the figure is 58 percent and goes to 63 percent for African-Americans. In a society that places a high value on skills, the educational system is condemning many minority children to second class status. The practice of this fraud on the public is the disguised work of what Mr. Edwards calls the soft bigotry of low expectations. He brings it home by reporting the results of Achieve Minneapolis, the Minneapolis Public Schools Title I department. The reading advocates noted that in 2002, 70 percent of sixth graders at a North Minneapolis school came in reading at the third grade level.[9]

The Way's Educational Alternative

The Way offered a tutorial program critical of educational efforts that promoted idealistic images that have little reality in the everyday world particularly for African-American young people. **The Way** offered an alternative approach for public schools on how to act as a counterweight to the surrounding society. **The Way** educators never told young people what they already knew, but rather focused on helping them to imagine alternative futures, alternatives the larger society cannot imagine but needs. **The Way** offered this extraordinary gift to its students by imparting the desire to be disciplined free persons equipped to function in a complex world that does not always deal from the top of the deck. **The Way** had the insight and the know-how in turning around a skeptical temper of mind that believed nothing it is told to show the advantage one gains in engaging life with a healthy critical attitude. **The Way** took advantage of students' brashness by turning it into a critical temper that asks the relevant questions and insists on pertinent answers. Thus **The Way** sought to transform the educational task in reaching students of color by delivering the young from soft-headedness, influenced by hard circumstance, into hard thinking. So it became the task of **The Way** educators to melt the cold heart, that saw too much that is cruel, by their own warmth of empathy that is never mistaken for anything but a real attitude toward the living of life. **The Way's** imaginative pedagogical gift imparted dynamic motives that makes every student, seen as a little prophet, a fellow worker in the creative social struggle that is demanded if all are to be fully free.

Taking It Another Step—Criminalizing the Criminal: Prisons as Schools for Crime

It is commonly understood by the public, reinforced by prison movies, that one of the greatest causes of criminality in America is the penal system. Criminologists know prisons become schools for crime. Irving Goffman made it clear over forty years ago that prisons are "total institutions."[10] Their intent is to strip an individual of any previous identity and re-socialize them as a new personality that belongs in the new institutional setting. Here one learns how one is defined as a criminal. Evil is the other, as I wrote in the chapter on Ishmael. And guess what, behind bars one soon assumes the identity of Ishmael, the other.

The current system deals with criminals by demanding retribution. America wants criminals to pay for what they have done. The public wants the courts to exact an eye for an eye and a tooth for a tooth. Those who been victimized, those who have lost loved ones to perpetrators that take life without a wink, want no mercy and so reinforce public sentiment.

Oddly enough, the public's desire for retribution is tied to the hope that severe punishment will act as a deterrent to committing future crimes. The outcome is that punishment does not produce what society believes it should. Our penal system does not deter crime as it simply warehouses people to keep them out of circulation. All one need do is look at the statistics of repeat offenders, we quickly learn that putting criminals in jail does little or nothing to deter them from future criminal acts.

The Way's Neighborhood Probationary Counseling Project

The Criminal Justice System forty years ago, as it is today, was showing a high rate of recidivism. Willie Mae Dixon, **The Way's** community worker, saw what was happening and knew something had to be done. She had seen in the vast majority of cases that the probation system is inadequate to the task. The system was not only understaffed but lacked a workable knowledge of the many persons of color that were coming through the system. Forty years ago most probation officers were White and had little affinity and even less knowledge of African-Americans.

Offenders of color that appeared in court to be placed on probation would often appear again. This repetitive pattern was only interrupted by a jail sentence. Ms. Dixon saw such patterns as a failure by the community as well as a system charged with extending corrective supervision to all who had broken the law.

The Way, under her leadership, developed a program to address the needs particularly of young African-American offenders. Willie Mae understood that the young offender often underwent an incomprehensible experience of arrest and trial at the hands of people one did not trust. Society works on the assumption that the rude awakening of an arrest and court trial is sufficient to implant a sense of civility. It often works the opposite on young African-American men. The system assumes offenders will take the initiative in seeking probation officers out, but often they did not. Willie Mae Dixon knew that traversing the territory of the law was totally foreign to young persons of color. She also knew the system did not encourage family support. In many cases, the family does not have the ability to help. In other cases, the family may have just given up. This leaves the professional probation officer, who has little time to give, the only contact. To make matters worse, probation officers are viewed by the probationer, as Willie Mae only could say, "an epilogue of officialdom," one who is not concerned with an individual's best interests. **The Way's** Neighborhood Probationary Project sought to fill this gap by becoming not simply a friend of the court but a friend of the offender.[11]

The Way staff, under the leadership of Willie Mae Dixon, started this pioneer program by employing residents from the African-American community to serve as counselors. Their job was to meet and work with juvenile and adult offenders assigned to the project by the courts. The project represented a shift in the methods of probationary treatment as it utilized persons born and raised in the same environment, struggling with the same issues as the offenders. Some counselors had done time and had started a new life. This was no simple thing. It was a revolutionary concept in 1967 to have neighborhood people working side by side with probation officers. An evaluation took place over a period of two years. Evaluation of success was based on tangible signs of progress such as length of residence and job stability. There were also intangible signs of progress that the counselors, due to their background, could detect and interpret to the benefit of those needing help.

Here a prescription went beyond the common knowledge and description of a growing ill. It is a good sign that society at times can benefit from the past and so build on it for the betterment of future generations. The Neighborhood Probationary Counseling Project was a precursor to the development of Neighborhood Restorative

Justice Centers in the African-American community, a prescription to restore the offending individual back to the community, a prescription as old as Moses.

Recreating the Biblical Model of Restorative Justice

One need not draw out all the influences of the Judeo-Christian community on the development of prisons. One would suffice. The name penitentiary is sufficient to show that prison is more than a warehouse for prisoners but a place of penitence, of moral and soul correction. What became lost over the years was the initial model devised at the foot of Sinai for people who had escaped from slavery. The people had come out, come out of a place of corporate wealth where the powerful controlled all the public processes, come out of a place where little ones were used up and discarded and where weak ones were abused and oppressed, come out of the land of Pharaoh that had coerced and silenced marginal ones. When asked how they came out, all they could do was to sing and dance.

At Sinai the Decalogue, the Ten Commandments, were given. It was God's no to wannabe Pharaohs. No other gods. No graven images. No wrongful use of the name of God.

The voice from Mount Sinai moves from divine holiness to the creation of human community. Keep the Sabbath. Honor parents. No killing. No adultery. No stealing. No crooked courts. No acquisitive coveting. "Thou shalt nots" are God's restraint to the works that work for nil, for nothing, for death. God's no stood against those seeking personal advantage that endangered the community, God's neighborhood.

Moses explains the significance of God's commandments and its impact on human community in the biblical book known as Deuteronomy. One could call it "God's Neighbor Book."[12] It is the socio-economic-political vision for vulnerable ones. The God who commands powers, angels, and principalities is mightily concerned with orphans, widows, and strangers. Orphans because they have no daddy and widows because they have no husband in a patriarchal society, strangers because they have no community to protect them.

God is mightily concerned where there is no daddy, no parent, no bread winner, no advocate, no protector, leaving the vulnerable exposed to the devouring power of the ruthless. The stranger today is under the threat of being disenfranchised, red-lined from getting loans, kept down by glass ceilings, the undocumented worker whose life consists of standing around with seasonal or occasional jobs, a life of endless anxiety over visas, a person without vistas.

Let us examine God's Neighbor Book to see more clearly the radical teaching implied in the practice of neighborliness. The teaching is about the year of release. It is tied to the Year of Jubilee, the fiftieth year when all debts are forgiven, all persons sold to pay a debt come home, a time when all land taken as a payment of debt is returned to its original owner.

This was an extraordinary requirement to assure there would be no permanent underclass in the neighborhood, no continual line of disadvantaged people. This upset conventional economic patterns that kept people in debt and so changed it as to bring creditor and debtor together in a neighborly way, to curb the power of the creditor in order to limit the hurt or indignity to debtors. In God's Neighbor-Hood, power relationships are brought into the covenantal fabric of neighborliness.

In God's Neighbor-Hood, unlike Monopoly where the object of the game is to bankrupt the other players, the community must keep releasing people from debt, keep breaking vicious cycles of indebtedness and power in order to have a neighborhood. The year of release is the Sabbath principle that maintains God's Neighbor-Hood. The Sabbath is a time for God's Neighbor-Hood to rest, relax, and find peace, to break the vicious cycle of consumption and production; God's Neighbor-Hood deploys power differently in order to have a neighborhood.

This brings us back to corrections, penitence, and payment for so-called debts owed to society. Forgiveness in the Bible is about economics in the first instance. The primal forgiveness is of debts, all other forgiveness follows. So the "year of release" is about debt forgiveness as the basic condition for God's Neighbor-Hood. There are four things sought in the biblical model for dealing with crime (debt owed) that involve the steps of restitution, repentance, reconciliation, and restoration.

In biblical times, the first thing required of a guilty party was that restitution be made to compensate the victim of a crime. Zaccheus is the story of a tax collector who repents of cheating people and immediately he makes restitution to those from whom he has stolen.[13] He not only pays back what he has stolen but much more is returned, as prescribed by the law that demanded victims of robbery be paid back four times over what was stolen. Zaccheus joyfully paid it and is restored to his community.

Think how things have changed in contemporary society. Many young thieves do not know how hard it is to earn money. Many, when asked about the store they stole from, simply shrug their shoulders saying, "They're rich. Besides, their insurance company will cover their losses." What the young person hasn't figured out is where does the insurance company get its money but from the hard-working policyholders whose higher premiums cover the losses from robberies.

What is needed is to have those who commit crimes against property to work it off, to bring restitution to the person who has suffered the loss. One can't do that in prison. Making restitution is a form of penitence, to restore what was undone. Presently, paying a debt to society means nothing but doing time and getting rehabilitated. To someone one has robbed, paying a debt, means learning the value of being a neighbor, as well as the value of work, and can lead to restoring the thief back into the community. The person may learn a trade or a vocation in the process so as not to be economically disadvantaged when he or she is released.

Reconciliation is key to being part of God's Neighbor-Hood, part of the community. Reconciliation cannot happen without confrontation, without bringing the thief and the person who has been robbed together in some meaningful way. The present judicial/penal system keeps them apart as a rule. It is important for the victim to have a face-to-face encounter with the thief. This can promote healing for it puts a face on the victim as well as puts a face on the criminal. Until there is guilt, there can be no repentance, and without repentance there can be no restoration. In God's Neighbor-Hood, both the victim and the victimizer are brought together into a relationship that seeks to be redemptive to both.

Restorative Justice Centers In African-American Communities

Presently there are a million and more men and women in American prisons and the numbers are expected to grow. Already the ratio of African-American males to European-American males is 27:1 in the state of Minnesota. Since prisons are more often than not a school for criminals, society will be releasing even greater numbers of criminals who will most likely commit more crime.

Prisons are overcrowded. Too often state and city governments lack money to build more prisons to keep up with demand. Private prisons are now being created that has attracted investors and entrepreneurs. The time has come to create Restorative Justice Centers in African-American communities that build on the spiritual wisdom and experience of the community.

Restorative Justice Centers would initially be for those convicted of nonviolent crimes as well as for the young. The centers would extend the work of the "Restorative Justice/Peacemaking Circles," initially brought to Minnesota from Canada where they have been used in Native American communities.[14] Now centers perform the work of justice and reconciliation under the auspices of such groups as the North Minneapolis Community Justice Committee.

The benefits such centers could bring to individuals and the African-American community will in itself be an act of Jubilee, bringing their young home so they can be made whole again. The simple benefit of having the incarcerated in the neighborhood makes family contacts easier as it is non-disruptive to work and school schedules. It also makes possible the access to a pool of volunteers from religious and community groups that could be mentors to the young.

The promotion of jobs would be a benefit of work-release programs in the community. Worship services could be provided by community religious groups. Once a prisoner is released, he could be adopted by a religious group or family in the community who understand his situation and could help him through the difficult time of reentry to civilian life.

Restorative Justice Centers in the Twin Cities' African-American communities could actually become places where captives are set free. The strengths the community can offer will help inmates break the bonds of their captivity to a destructive lifestyle. That is its liberating promise that needs to become a reality.

We began this chapter with a quote from a jurist, Learned Hand. His remarks came two weeks before D-Day, the Allied invasion of Nazi Europe on June 6, 1944. The fight for freedom was at stake. Learned Hand, an important judge though not well known, was invited to speak at the annual festival in Central Park for the swearing in of 150,000 naturalized citizens.

The address became widely circulated in its day, even compared to Lincoln's Gettysburg Address. Judge Learned Hand offered a simple civic lesson that we, today, need to take to heart. The judge said, the spirit of liberty must never be arrogant for it must take into account the merits and needs of one's neighbor. Liberty means to weigh one's interests along side the interests of one's neighbor. The judge then said that the spirit of liberty is the spirit of Jesus who taught us that God's neighborhood is the place where the least are heard and considered of equal weight to those who are considered the greatest. Justice holds the balance between the interests of the weak over against the interests of the strong, a balance that secures neighborhoods where freedom thrives and people possess a future.

The Way Toward
Renewal Of Public Life
Glenwood-Lyndale Redevelopment

Threat to the Republic:
Loss of Public Life

We live in a world where we are all strangers. Public life involves strangers who interact and come together through various ways—on street corners, at museums and cafes, wherever strangers gather. Public life is important for a republic such as ours. Humans have always found places of common life where feeling and thinking people can debate and decide issues important to their daily lives. However, public life has fallen on difficult days. Without public life, politics becomes a theater of illusion. Everyone watches what is on stage, some hoping to get a part to play, a piece of the action, while the real action goes on backstage in the raw exercise of unchecked power. Public life is the basis of community that, in turn, establishes government and makes it accountable to the people.[1]

We Know The Way:
Philosophy of Community Reform

[Mahmoud El-Kati wrote an essay on philosophy of reform that expressed **The Way's** *approach toward the building of community. The following is an excerpt from the essay written in 1968.]*

This is a new day and we need a new way. **The Way** unabashedly assumes the role of being a part of the new mood in quest for a people oriented rather than a thing and/or racist oriented society. Thus, in the first stage of **The Way's** development, we prefer to be movement oriented rather than organization oriented. It is not so much where you stand, but in which direction you are going. To be an organization means to be institutionalized, which means an established, sterile, overly-objective, pragmatic, anti-philosophical, anti-cultural, one-eyed way of looking at and dealing with human life.[2]

The Way's Community Training Program

The Way possessed the hard-headed realism of Saul Alinsky who had organized the poor in Chicago during the forties into the sixties. Alinksy said power moved between two poles—those who've got the money and those who've got the people.[3] **The Way**, like Alinksy, didn't have the money so it sought to organize the people to gain control over their own community.

The heart of **The Way's** philosophy of community reform was to convince people they could do something for themselves. The challenge was to show how people could participate in the building of new vehicles for social reform. **The Way** sought to imaginatively challenge people so they would find ways to exercise power in reshaping their community. **The Way's** Community Training Program became the tool to do just that.

The community training staff was made up of persons who were African-American, Native American, Jew, and White European. Forty-nine workers were employed the summer of 1967 that included persons from the community working alongside college students.

The Way's community trainers went door to door, block by block in all directions. Two surveys were taken of the community. The first asked householders the type of housing desired in the community, with an income breakdown of residents; the other survey was geared toward the social service needs of the community. The surveys were presented to the Housing Authority, city officials, and Pilot City Health Center personnel.

Both surveys were an effort to get residents involved in making decisions about themselves. Questions were asked regarding problems as seen by residents of the Near North Side and what they wanted to see done about them. Persons were encouraged to come to **The Way** to join others who also wanted to see these same problems solved. The challenge was to get one person from each household to be involved in one of the programs that were created by other residents along with the staff of **The Way**. Persons signed up for work groups, called commissions, that included education, law enforcement, economic development, community involvement, youth action, medical aid, housing, and religious unity.

These work commissions brainstormed and created new programs in response to the needs expressed by residents from the door-to-door interviews. The only commission never to get off the ground was religious unity that Orpheus Williams and I co-chaired. A general unwillingness greeted us among ministers on the Near North Side to become directly involved with **The Way**.

However, **The Way's** Community Training Program did spawn a women's club rummage sale, pap smear clinic, a drop-in credit union, a movie theater and a drama group that staged several plays, adult education classes, college orientation classes, GED preparation, and scholarship committee. A whirlwind of activity swept across the community during the summer of 1967, which was largely the result of a few persons who went door to door to get people involved. Such efforts by **The Way** involved people in making choices that effected their lives as well as to discover how persons working together with a common goal can begin to build community.

Bringing It Home for the Homeless: Glenwood-Lyndale Redevelopment Or the Hollman [Dis]Accords

Glenwood-Lyndale Redevelopment Plan, known as the Hollman Accords, involved tearing down "The Projects," as low-income housing on Near North Side was called. The Projects was one of the first efforts by the federal government to provide public housing. In 1939, public housing in Minneapolis was built only for Whites. Public housing in Minneapolis was integrated in 1941 through the strong efforts of Nellie Stone Johnson and the League of Negro Women. Nellie Stone was a powerful conscience and fighter for equality in Minneapolis and, with the help of the league, found an ally in Mary McCloud Bethune. Ms. Bethune was an African-American activist and close friend of Eleanor Roosevelt. Mrs. Roosevelt encouraged her husband and American president to mandate integration for public housing on the Near North Side of Minneapolis. Fifty-five years later public leaders said The Projects had to go declaring the concept of concentrated low-income housing was as outdated as the buildings.

The Hollman Accords was an example where the best of intentions turned bad. However, good intentions do not necessarily make for wise political choices particularly where there is little regard for the people who had to move from their homes.[4] The Hollman Accords were initially a collaborative creation involving the city of Minneapolis, HUD (Housing and Urban Development), Legal Aid, and the Minneapolis NAACP. The consent decree put the Glenwood-Lyndale Redevelopment Plan in motion to move seven hundred and seventy low income families of color out of North Minneapolis and, presumably, years later, to allow two hundred and twenty of those families to return and benefit from an upgrade in their housing. That was 1995.

Then things changed on an early September day in 1999. A group calling themselves the Hollman 14, made up of North Side clergy and residents, were arrested. The group protested the demolition of homes of low-income families and by standing in the path of a bulldozer were arrested for trespassing. The reason given for the protest was because no suitable housing existed for the families being displaced.

Public leaders derogatorily referred to the protestors, such as "Despite what you might have seen and heard from a handful of protestors," and "amidst all the curbside press conferences."[5] It was clear in the eyes of certain public leaders the protestors were a small minority of rabble-rousers, not to be taken seriously, whose resistance made governing more difficult than those who govern might like.

Certain public leaders put their cards on the table. Comments by Carol Batsell Benner, commissioner of Minneapolis Public Housing Authority, State Representative Gregory Gray, and Matthew Ramadan, executive director of the Northside Residents Redevelopment Council, made their position clear. "Expert testimony before the focus group charged with devising a redevelopment plan supported the contention that only by demolishing these distressed housing developments and creating a new mixed-income community could we greatly reduce, if not eliminate, the poverty entrenched in this neighborhood."[6]

These seemingly benign words "only by demolishing" and the sterile addition "greatly reduce, if not eliminate, the poverty entrenched" reminds one of the American officer's notorious remark made in the heat of the Vietnam War after torching a small village; "We have to destroy the village to save it." The public leaders' words had an eerie feeling and, I believe, though unimagined, nonetheless, were like gasoline thrown on the fire that heated the debate over the Glenwood-Lyndale Redevelopment Plan. Ron Edwards, no stranger to North Side politics, wryly described the Hollman Accords as a "half-baked project, a failure in time. . .a Hollywood back lot of facades with no substance behind them for minorities."[7]

At stake was the role of public life as it mediates between the individual and the powers of government. A healthy public life makes healthy politics possible, first by showing how the public protects the individual from political manipulation, then by showing how it empowers the individual to play a political role. These two ingredients were conspicuously absent in the Glenwood-Lyndale Redevelopment agreement.

Reverend Curtis Herron, one of the Hollman 14, responded with words that would prove prophetic. He described city policy toward low-income citizens, particularly persons of color, "We don't want you here—get out of town."[8] He went on to charge public leaders in using "the Hollman Consent Decree as pseudo-legal justification for institutional racism and classism. They seek not to reduce poverty, but to move the poor around or out of the city entirely to attract more upper income suburbanites."[9] That is just what happened. An article in the *Star Tribune* a few years later carried the headline "Housing Settlement Misses Its Mark."[10] Suburbanites and middle class had indeed taken residence where once the poor dwelt. And what of the poor? Scattered about and largely forgotten. What was promised was never delivered; they were served notice they could not move back.[11]

Reverend Herron's words had sadly come true. "Hollman is also being used to justify a ban against the construction of any new affordable housing in so-called 'concentrated' areas of the city. While decree proponents claim this will spur development, they know perfectly well that not only most suburbs but also eight of Minneapolis thirteen wards have no intention of allowing that to happen to any significant degree."[12] The *Star Tribune* article's closing line confirmed what Reverend Herron had said, "…some of the public housing meant for the suburbs may end up in the core cities after all."[13]

A Brookings Institute "Mind the Gap" report released in late 2005 revealed Minneapolis is, by income, the nation's second most segregated metropolitan city. Only Milwaukee's central city that is more disportionately poor, and its suburbs more disportionately rich, is more segregated.[14] Good intentions behind the notion concentrated low-income housing was outdated proved feeble against more stubborn realities and a disaster to those whose lives were uprooted.

Keeping the Republic Alive:
Creating Public People

When Alex de Tocqueville visited the youthful United States in the early nineteenth century, the Frenchman noted we were a nation of joiners. Everywhere he looked people were banding together in voluntary associations to share common interest, to accomplish common goals, to express a common faith. And de Tocqueville saw, with uncommon insight, that if the American experiment in democracy were to succeed, it would require the continued health of these voluntary associations. They were crucial forms of public life because a republic such as the United States requires some way of defending the isolated individual against the tendency of government to grow larger, stronger, and more domineering. He saw what has continued since the days of Pharaoh—any power, even in a democratic state, wants to enlarge its domain. So it gravitates toward controlling the thought and behavior of every individual in the society—an impossible goal, but one toward which power is ineluctably drawn. The individual who possesses conscience and freedom of thought and action is often perceived as anathema to the determination of political institutions.

History offers numerous examples of power's tendency to expand its own domain, totalitarian societies so-called because of their success in achieving near-total control. One characteristic of such a society is the managing of public life to be supportive of government. The destruction of settings where individuals can come out of isolation to become something greater than themselves are viewed as a threat to the ruling elite. For the individual who has a public life is suddenly more than an individual. He or she is now a member of a body, a part of an organic whole. To get people to stand up and protest transforms them from being a mere cog in the machinery to a more complete human being. Central power, however diffuse in its collaborations with various groups, finds it far more difficult to manipulate and manage such corporate beings than dealing with isolated individuals who have no such memberships.

Those who are caught up with large goals often fall to the dangerous practice of justifying the means by its own ends. The enthusiasm of such a mind-set was articulated by public leaders themselves, "Everyone involved—including the handful of protesters—has the same goal: improving the Glenwood-Lyndale neighborhood and building more affordable housing in the city."[15] There is much truth in such a bold inclusive statement; it is beguiling in that many good intentions overrode the individual participation of those most affected who lived in the Glenwood-Lyndale neighborhood. It is a profound mistake to exclude any person for any reason, for that fact alone not only diminishes public life, it dehumanizes such persons. The very fact that this personal reality has gone largely unnoticed shows how blind people of preconceived good intent have become, over time, in underestimating the value of persons assuming a strong role in public life. The naked loss of such persons participating in their own destiny, itself the high standard of a democracy if not the very foundation of freedom, is incalculable.

Rediscovering The Way

The Way sought to put into practice what had been understood in the Civil Rights Movement and was then being championed by proponents of Black Power—that an empowered people would be a powerful guide and check on government in seeking to make power accountable to the issues of justice. **The Way** leadership knew that isolated individuals are impotent to resist the imposition of governmental power and are powerless to direct established power in its course.

When people band together in a public setting, as the handful of clergy and protesters did in protest to the displacement of the poor and people of color who lived in The Projects, several kinds of empowerment occurred. Most obviously, a voice arose that had not been heard, even if it was only a child who recognized that the Emperor wears no clothes. It was key that numbers count. Multiplying the loaves and fishes into a feeding of thousands, as Jesus did, becomes a collective voice, a voice that can be heard above the machinery of government; those in positions of power who have a hard time hearing often listen up when the voice of protest goes public. As people participate in public life, their numbers not only add up, but also multiply. For as people participate, they gain confidence and competence in the skills required to function in public, skills that develop like mustard seeds in unlikely and insignificant settings that soon grow to larger fields of public concern.

However, what was missing in the Hollman dispute was an organization that offered empowerment to the people who lived in public housing and were most directly affected as their homes were threatened by the wrecking ball. The Hollman 14 spoke on the behalf of the residents. There were organizations and governmental agencies that knew what was best for these citizens. Yet, in **The Way's** absence, there was no advocate, no organization that sought to organize the public housing residents to speak in public with one voice; rather they were left to find their own path along the margins of survival.

There are lessons to be learned here. First, events that arouse public interest often threaten to bring diverse elements of the population into more frequent contact. The irony underlying the Glenwood-Lyndale redevelopment debate was that it proposed diversity; that was why most groups went along with the plan unmindful of its full impact, though it did not finally yield diversity.

Second, events occur only sporadically while public life is a continuing affair. Public life depends on regular encounters—most of them not overtly political—between strangers who cross each other's paths, become accustomed to each other's presence, and come to recognize their common claims on society. When the balance of life shifts heavily toward the private and these regular encounters diminish, people come into the public arena only in moments of crisis, moments that usually set stranger against stranger in sudden and unexpected conflicts of interest. The danger is that there is an inverse relation between the health of public life and the need to conduct politics by crisis. Where there is little public life, conflicts more likely will reach the crisis point before they are dealt with.

Third, the way conflicts are framed, such as the Glenwood-Lyndale redevelopment debate, can make or break public life. Usually, society defines such conflicts as zero-sum games in which each gain for one side is a loss to the other. It is a game where there is only one winner. Is it inconceivable in this republic we can seek to address public issues where everyone might emerge with a victory of some sort? A genuine public life would begin with the premise that there are victories for the whole that are greater than any victories of the parts. We would understand that we are members of one another, that the social order will be secure in the pursuit of life, liberty, and happiness only if all its persons are made secure by the same rights. We would know that when society forces low-income housing out of one community, we are not solving the problem, but merely postponing the day of reckoning. Worse still, we are allowing the pressures of inequity and resentment to build to a point where no rational solution will suffice. The foundation of public life lies in the tenacious faith that we are in this together and only together can we find ways for everyone to win some measure of dignity and respect.

The Glenwood-Lyndale Redevelopment Plan showed us that many hold to a faith that was preached often enough, but seldom put to good practice. There must be a community voice, like **The Way**, that will advocate such practical social change beyond institutional expectations. As Mahmoud El-Kati observed nearly forty years ago, "Obsolete or irrelevant institutions must be challenged. The moral contradictions in American life must be heightened. The contradictions must be put in full view of the people so that they might arrive at intelligent decisions and take charge of their own lives."[16]

Community or Chaos

The crisis on the Near North Side is an old and familiar story. Since the days of **The Way** there have been no comprehensive methods for community reform on the North Side of Minneapolis. **The Way** began the necessary research and education that involved the community in its own regeneration. [read Appendix II] The fact its prototype has never been practiced by others, or refined and perfected by further experimentation, reveals the failure of will and of vision. A revolution of values still looks warily on the growing divide between the powerless and those with power.

The Way People Can
Speak To Power

Board of The Way and
Greater Minneapolis Urban Coalition

A general idea is always a danger to the existing order.

—A. N. Whitehead[1]

The Way Board of Directors:
Participating Democrats and Enlightened Plutocrats

The December *Minneapolis Tribune* Sunday feature magazine was devoted exclusively to **The Way**.[2] It highlighted the tangible and the intangible benefits of **The Way's** board of directors. The tangible support came from fund-raising accurately reported as "that kind of support has freed **The Way** from the kind of accountability a United Way agency has to have in terms of success in its programs. It has allowed **The Way** to assume a kind of independence in their dealings with other agencies both on the North Side and in the Negro community."[3] The intangible involved "access to the creative, imaginative people around other institutions patronized by the wealthy—The Walker Art Center, Minneapolis Institute of Arts, and the Tyrone Guthrie Theater."[4]

The Way's board of directors influenced the ongoing direction of **The Way** as the board transformed itself into a major player in its own right. It was a role the board did not initially choose but found itself playing as it had to deal with the various issues and crises that came time and again. It became clear, after the first few months, that the board would not be making policy and then going home. The traditional role of a board of directors would not work at **The Way**. Board members needed to roll up their sleeves and get involved by encouraging and working alongside staff in the various work areas of the organization. The board of **The Way** became one of advise and consent as it interfaced with staff in forging the program direction about the social issues and personal needs faced day to day. The board of directors became a forum for public debate over the impending issues of the day. Here board members and staff, often with members of the community present, would debate issues and make difficult decisions as they sought to direct **The Way** between the Scylla of provocation and the Charybdis of appeasement.

The makeup of the board in its first four years held a wide spectrum of opinions and backgrounds. Wealth sat next to the poor, big business sat next to neighborhood business owners, Protestant and Catholic clergy sat next to each other. The Jewish community was well represented by persons who once lived on the Near North Side and some who owned businesses there. There were college professors and lawyers, socialists and republicans, democrats and some that had no party affiliation but simply were involved persons who were concerned for justice. It was an assembly of people from many walks of life, a microcosm of society, that constituted **The Way** board of directors of thirty-some members.

Wealth was represented by Louise McCannel, a member of the Walker family after which the Walker Art Center is named, along with Sage Cowles, a member of the Cowles family that owned the *Star* and *Tribune* newspapers at the time, and Penny Winton whose family's Minnetonka chateau now serves as Cargill's corporate office.

People from the community came to be part of **The Way** board in the persons of Mary Bible, Earby Chatham, Rosa Clark, Pauline Parks, and Pat Bendsten. Leaders from the Black community included Josie Johnson, who traveled to Mississippi to visit the Freedom Schools in the dangerous mid-sixties, Joe Buckhalton, a director at Twin Cities Opportunities Industrial Center (TCOIC), along with Edward Pillow who was the director of Moblization of Economic Resources (MOER). Spike Moss and Clarence Bedford represented Black youth.

Labor was represented by Frank Alsup, and Doug Hall was the lawyer on the board. Michael Gaines represented the city as director of the mayor's commission on human relations. Big business was represented by Ray Plank, Gordon Ritz, and Max Fallek, while neighborhood businesses were represented by Odell Livingston, who ran a corner gas station on Plymouth Avenue, along with Theodore Desnik, who owned the corner drugstore on Plymouth and Penn.

Along with Fallek and Desnik, several persons from the Jewish community became involved from the very start—Joyce Kahn, Kurt Kaufman, and Miram Cohn. University of Minnesota faculty were involved in the persons of David Cooperman, a professor of sociology, along with Gerald Lee, a physician who was on the faculty of the University's School of Medicine. Then there was Thomas Johnson, one of the few Black physicians in the city, who operated a clinic on Plymouth Avenue. Other board members included Gerald Viznor, a Native American and newspaper journalist who became a well-known writer, along with Dennis Wynne, a social worker who worked with Syl Davis at Wells Memorial.

Reverend Orpheus Williams, whose storefront church on Plymouth Avenue was burned down in the summer of 1966, along with Reverend James Ware, represented Black clergy. Catholic clergy was represented by Father James Schuller, as the Protestant clergy included Reverends Williams and Ware, Merle Carlson, and Knox Seaton from the Baptist, Lutheran, and Presbyterian churches respectively, along with myself, a Methodist.

The Way board of directors was an extraordinary amalgam of persons that performed a pioneering work in a very demanding hour in our city's history. They came together in the belief that their work would bring dignity and a semblance of justice to people too often forgotten and neglected. The board's greatest intangible evolved as it became an experiment in the way people can address power.

What was unique about this board was that it brought to a common table two poles of society—the powerful and those growing in power. I was fond of saying, in those amazing days, that **The Way** brought together the participating democrats and the plutocrats. We saw a new mood coming to enthrall marginalized groups, transforming them into participating democrats. No longer were people sitting on the sidelines; rather they demanded a role with those who made the rules of the game. Various sectors of society learned their lessons through the labor and civil rights movements, lessons continually taught to those in the peace and women's movements of the ways to effectively exercise power—these groups became the emerging participating democrats. The plutocrats were powerful because of their wealth. There is no aristocracy in the United States unless it is supported by wealth that translates itself into power. What came as a surprise was that some of the most radical board members were plutocrats. "...most of the wealthy members of the board seem able to 'swing' with what **The Way** is doing more easily than some of the others."[5]

Those who could not live with such a demanding board soon resigned. A few resigned over disagreements with controversial items printed in **The Way** newspaper. However, two key board resignations marked the passage the board sailed between the rocks and hard places as it faced the difficult issues communities of growing power must confront.

The resignation of Ray Plank, a businessman and one of the key supporters of **The Way**, had its impact and was duly noted by the *Tribune*.

> Plank, for instance, resigned from the board in September, but the way he did it suggested he disagreed more with the way it operated than with **The Way**. He took pains to keep his resignation secret as long as possible to minimize whatever negative effect on fund-raising his departure might have. And he promised **The Way** his continued support, but in other ways, not as a director."[6]

As I reread Ray's resignation letter years later, I realized he had come to the understanding that **The Way** was becoming an advocate of Black Power, which he believed was not its original mandate. He could not be party to such a direction; however, he would not seek to dictate by saying in public that it was the wrong direction to take. He observed, "that such advocacy would bring division within the very community **The Way** sought to serve."[7]

The second key resignation was Dr. Thomas Johnson. I had been quoted to say that the position taken by the board during the Lincoln Junior High controversy [recapitulated below] did not damage the board.[8] I was wrong. The loss of the voices of Thomas Johnson and Ray Plank that came as a result of that conflict did damage **The Way** board in the eyes of differing communities.

The Lincoln Junior High Slapping Incident

The first major test of the board came when a White teacher at Lincoln Junior High slapped a Black student just before Christmas break in 1967. The incident turned into an attack on **The Way**. The second newspaper editorial on the Lincoln incident sets the debate rather accurately.

> "They can close us down if they want, but there will still be **The Way** if we have to meet out on the street." This impassioned statement last week at a meeting in **The Way** community center of North Minneapolis came not from a Black power youth, but from a Negro mother with a child in Lincoln Junior High.
>
> The day before, leaders of a group called Concerned North Side Residents were calling **The Way** a cancer that has infected the area. This disease, it was said, must either be cured or eradicated. **The Way** became an issue in the Lincoln Junior High controversy, and it will continue to be an issue in the community as long as it represents the militancy of the "have-nots" as against the moderation of the "haves." Other cities have their ways, too, but they are submerged in big-

ger problems. Here the visibility is high, and the controversy great, and the issue will not go away until the problems of race and poverty go away.[9]

The irony of the slapping incident was when **The Way**, seeking to serve as a mediator between the school and the community, came under attack from a group called Concerned North Side Residents (CNR). CNR called for a boycott of the school by Black parents to keep their children out of school. Richard Parker was CNR's chair and spokesperson. Parker's feelings were expressed in hyperbole when he stated "98 percent of the people of the Near North Side oppose **The Way's** administration."[10] Parker accused **The Way** leadership in using "the children as pawns and the downtrodden as pawns. They don't give a damn about the poor."[11] Then he went on to call **The Way** a "White man's establishment" noting that much of its financial support came from White business such as Raymond Plank, president of Apache Corporation. Mrs. Dan Luce, a member of CNR, drove the point home by saying, "If these people [supporters of **The Way**] lived in the area they would change their tune immensely. Plank has never seen the seamy side of life."[12]

Since the controversy was taking place just before Christmas break, the Minneapolis Board of Education decided the wisest policy was to close the school early and let things cool off.

I had written to Dr. John Davis, the superintendent of schools, that "the 'hot week' before Christmas should serve as a reminder to us that we must never again permit ourselves to be so divided in understanding and so separated in communication."[13]

The Way board met on December 19. We found ourselves well divided as to what to do and in great disagreement whether or not to support the boycott. This was the first significant test as to the amenability of the board. There was a limit to the slack board members needed to give those they disagreed with.

Dr. Johnson would not let the board off easily. For him it was a defining issue. He was adamant that the habit of institutional obeisance be broken. He was in favor of having parents and students boycott the school; anything less would be kowtowing to people of wealth.

What would be the position of the board? Doug Hall was delighted with the controversy, for it offered new opportunities to define what **The Way** was all about. He supported Syl Davis who had shown he was a master in dealing with such difficult situations. The board need not put a straight jacket on the director's work. Besides, Doug Hall said, "White members of the board were not qualified to speak on this issue." He offered this warning. "If the board did not support the boycott, a good portion of the community would only believe that **The Way** was supporting the school system." However, **The Way** had initially sought to be conciliatory rather than confrontational. Some voices on the board supported this action. Some thought this was a more comprehensive approach to the problem for the schools would open again, and how would **The Way** be seen after all the smoke had settled? Then again some, like Dr. Johnson, saw this as a betrayal of the original purpose of **The Way** as an advocate for people who, far too often, suffer insults from institutional racism.

It became apparent to me certain board members were seeking a clarification as to the role of the board regarding issues of controversy. Should **The Way,** represented by its board and its staff, take sides, or was it to be a voice for the entire community? What if the board and staff were at opposite poles? Articles from the bylaws were quoted by members of the board to the effect that the purpose of **The Way** was "to bring together all residents of the community, regardless of ethnic origin, color, age, sex, or other traditionally separating out techniques so as to train and educate them for the purpose of improving and developing their talents and capabilities."[14] The argument was leading to the conclusion that should the organization not enjoy the support of the community, it would die. Again, certain voices spoke up in support of the boycott. These voices were resisted because it meant **The Way** supported a small segment of the community that would not stop short in getting their way. Doctor Johnson stood defiant.

He would support Black leaders who called for the school boycott, as they were being led by Bill Smith and Matt Eubanks—-whom he believed were sincere in their motives.

It was at this point Syl Davis spoke his mind. He said, "One of the basic problems the board and staff is dealing with is honesty. Honesty is required, not simply of those citizens involved, but of a community and its various interested leaders who fail to face the underlying problem of racism." By implication, Syl was saying the CNR criticism of **The Way** came as a result of **The Way** having established a reputation for fighting for African-American males that CNR members believed were nothing but gangsters and a threat to the Near North Side community. Syl was seeking to help the board understand this issue was not a popularity contest between North Side groups. This was a contest of wills: Would the will of Black and poor people be heard or the will of a dominant society, reflected by CNR (inferred by Syl but never said openly in deference to Dr. Johnson), that supported institutional restraint and control?

The situation had become polarized and so had the board. What should be the role of **The Way** in such a standoff? "It would be foolish," Doug Hall said, "to think we can make people understand if they don't want to." In polarized situations understanding is not what happens. Action is everything. While I was chairing the debate, I was handed a statement that I quickly read. I asked Louise McCannel if she had written it. She said, "I did." I presented Louise's statement to the board and, after lengthy debate, it was adopted. The genius of the statement was to go beyond the boycott in encouraging the school system to create "machinery for settling problems in mutually acceptable ways." A public statement was released to the press on December 23. The statement went to the underlying issues the board sought to deal with in an hour when **The Way's** solidarity with the community, let alone between the board and the staff, was most threatened.

American society today is racist despite declarations, laws, and words expressing good intentions. It still operates on the premise that its Black citizens are inferior to Whites. Many

Afro-Americans, particularly the young, will no longer abide by society's judgement that they are unworthy of full equality. They mean to do all they can to force that society to live up to its Judeo-Christian principles and to the democratic ideals expressed in our constitution.

At the same time, most Whites (and many Negroes) continue to be conditioned in a racist society, which, by its actions, reiterates in a thousand ways a conviction that the Negro's "place" in life is below that of any person with a White skin. This conditioning is so powerful that even the best-intentioned people unconsciously exhibit from time to time the strong prejudice bred into us by a basically racist environment.

Given the irresistible force of Afro-American determination pushing against the immovable mass of White racism, it is not surprising that Minneapolis North Side children should find themselves in conflict among themselves and with their teachers. This conflict, by testimony of minority parents and children, is as strong as other areas of Greater Minneapolis. It will not go away soon nor of itself.

We, the board of **The Way**—Opportunities Unlimited, Inc., request that the Minneapolis Department of Human Rights be invited by the Minneapolis School Board to analyze the manifestations of society's racial problems found city-wide in public education and to recommend the kind of machinery which will divert the energy generated by these problems into creative channels. This kind of machinery—student human relations groups, for example—should be designed not only to reduce immediate friction but also to enable students and faculty to help make the changes needed in our community to build a realistically just society for all.[15]

I sent the resolution along with a letter to Dr. David Preus, a fellow clergy and chairperson of the Minneapolis Board of Education. In the letter I called attention to the board's position that if the "machinery

for settling problems in mutually acceptable ways" would be acted
on by the school, then the boycott would no longer be needed. The
news hit the headlines—**The Way** urges the boycott to end. There was
immediate and contrary reactions from board members. The first was
Ray Plank, and the second was Dr. Thomas Johnson. Lines had been
drawn. Ray Plank wrote a letter to me immediately on reading the
paper, and I now wonder to what extent the remarks of CNR members about his role at **The Way**, privately conveyed, had affected him.

> I'm sorry the paper carried the particular headline Sunday
> on **The Way** urging the boycott be ended, for the text was con-
> ditional. And I understand some of the residents did feel they
> had been "sold out." Nonetheless, in terms of my contacts in
> the North Side, regrettably, there are many more who view **The
> Way** as a malignancy to be cut away from the society's anatomy
> and destroyed before the tumor further infects them.[16]

The conflict had brought out our ghosts and we had to deal with
them. Obviously, Ray had felt the discourse of the previous board
meeting had gone beyond civil bounds.

> Accordingly, in my view, the board and staff together must
> continue to seek mutuality of respect and understanding—
> which forces were pretty rampantly opposed Saturday. Again
> I feel we can make our greatest progress when the mortars
> aren't lobbing shells into enemy camps at close quarters.[17]

Ray was reeling from the repercussions of the debate. His voice
evidenced how a person of power perceives "being talked to if not
being accused."[18] Ray was intelligent and a voice that could not be dismissed in such debates. He goes on to write:

> I've expressed myself to school authorities on the need
> for them to initiate and cultivate contact with **The Way** dur-
> ing the remainder of the vacation [alluding to an important
> role he was playing behind the scenes], and now I'd like to
> suggest the counterpart. **The Way's** approach to the school
> system will not alone rest on pride and confrontation, but on

doing the less glamorous, but equally necessary, homework of seeking and discussing, backing it up with the very present need for change.[19]

It was clear in the public's mind, as Ray envisioned it, that **The Way** was seen to be the cause of trouble, not the school administrators who had called in the police, let alone the teacher who had slapped the student. We were down to the essentials of the working of power.

> Regarding the board-staff relationships, I do believe the board must risk that which I previously have shied away from lest the staff be dominated; namely, the dialogue out of which understanding must come. There is dissidence among board members, centering on the assertion that the executive committee and director are insensitive to many in the community whose interest at best, and neutrality [in the middle], have given way to anti-**Way** positions.[20]

Alluding to many in the community who were becoming critical of **The Way** was a voice Ray was in tune with, and he offered it as a warning, not a threat, for the benefit of **The Way**. It was a voice that needed to be discerned by members of the board and staff of **The Way**. Ray advocated for a strong board of directors. He wanted, as he said, "a single, constructive face, enabling the board to sell and take some heat off **Way** operating personnel."[21] Of course, this sounded like the corporate board room, for that was what Ray Plank was most familiar with. He understood such power and how it can best be used. He knew any enterprise must not jeopardize its relationship to its public. This was the underlining agenda for the next board meeting on January 2, 1968. The board again met and, after considerable debate, reaffirmed its position against the boycott by passing the following resolution.

> No child should be kept out of school or stay away from school as long as the opportunity for quality education and fair treatment exists. The school administration has responded constructively to the Parents Grievance Committee on the problem of police in the schools and the right of parents and

children to representation on grievances. We are hopeful that during the vacation period, specific solutions and long-range understanding can be arrived at between parents, children, and school officials. It is important that in this period plans for resuming the boycott be cancelled. It also important school officials recognize that deep problems exist, which must be worked out now, including the establishment of machinery for settling problems in mutually acceptable ways.

The Way is available to all, with or without problems and grievances, who seek our help in achieving solutions. We will make our facilities and ourselves available to all, regardless of disagreements on other issues. **The Way** has not and does not assume responsibility for what others say and do.[22]

On January 5, Lincoln Junior High School reopened. The teacher was reinstated. Dr. John Davis did seek to involve the Minneapolis Department of Civil Rights as well as Syl Davis and staff of **The Way** in developing machinery that would deal with racism within the schools. Seeking ways to create better relations between schools and the communities, **The Way** staff worked behind the scenes for many months. However, **The Way** lost a certain momentum, and its voice was muted in the community with the resignation of Dr. Thomas Johnson. A man of deep conviction, Dr. Johnson was well-known for his advocacy in the Black community. The board did not accept Dr. Johnson's resignation and asked him to return, but to no avail. The good doctor knew his mind and he had made it up. The loss of his voice on the board was a loss that could not be recaptured.

The board did not finally fulfill the promise of becoming a forum where people could address power. However, **The Way** board, in spite of its many failings, proved a significant effort that demonstrated the need for such public forums where people, from various communities of power interests, can listen and talk with each other and find the resolve to act in concert.

Speaking to Power: Urban Coalition of Minneapolis A General Assembly of Neighborhoods

It has been stated that the Urban Coalition
does not have the power for change within our city,
and that is sad indeed.
For if this body of men (and women)
does not have the power to bring about change within our city
in terms of a meaningful and effective method
towards the end of human dignity for Black people,
then I feel that all is lost."

—Syl Davis[23]

Louise McCannel writes of the early beginnings of the Greater Minneapolis Urban Coalition.

> After the second Plymouth Avenue explosion in July 1967, I became agitated enough about the local situation to ask fifteen businessmen to attend several emergency meetings to discuss a community-wide plan for realistically attacking race/poverty problems (and they were agitated enough to come.) . . .and subsequently [they] hired T. [Theatrice] Williams to help Larry Harris plan what became, in February 1968, the Minneapolis Urban Coalition.[24]

By September 12, 1967, Earl Ewald, president of Northern States Power (NSP) announced that a group of fourteen Minneapolis businessmen had engaged Larry Harris and Theatrice Williams for a nine-week period to study the practicality and need for an Urban Coalition of Minneapolis. Larry Harris was on the Minneapolis public school staff. Harris had secured a planning grant for a Human Relations Center as part of a three-year project under Title III of the Elementary and Secondary Education Act of 1965. T. Williams was the director of the well-known African-American Phyllis Wheatley Settlement House on the Near North Side.

The Urban Coalition had taken hold nationally under the leadership of John Gardner. President Lyndon Johnson convinced big business they were the saviors of the hour to address the racial unrest that erupted in nearly every major American city. Minneapolis was no exception, and so fourteen businessmen decided the city needed what would be called a "new level of integration, the integration of public and private resources in a well-planned and efficient-managed attack on the problem of poverty and race in Minneapolis."[25]

In early 1968, Syl Davis, Louise McCannel, and I were invited to become members of the Urban Coalition of Minneapolis. Syl would serve on the Executive Committee while Louise and I would be members of the Community Education Task Force chaired by Jim Bowe who proved to be an able and discerning leader. My invitation came from the coalition's first chairperson, Stephen Keating, president of Honeywell. He stated what he envisioned for the coalition.

> Above all else, we view the Coalition as a means of providing a dialogue, of improving communication and increasing understanding among all elements of our city. We need a commitment from all segments of our community to develop a city where every citizen is treated as a total human being.[26]

Keating had stated the importance of the Urban Coalition in creating a public forum for the voiceless. Before the first meeting of the Urban Coalition, I wrote a short essay entitled, "The Urban Coalition and The Poor," and sent it to the new coalition chair. I have edited and updated the essay for inclusion in this book.

> The moral implications of the relation of the poor and the Urban Coalition of Minneapolis are often overlooked or depreciated. The portion of our citizenship most anxious to express its loyalty to the principle of justice will be impatient with the limitations of the proposed Urban Coalition organization as an instrument of justice.

> When the Urban Coalition was informally launched in the fall of 1967, the readiness of many people welcomed it.

The coalition represented a new chapter in the spiritual pilgrimage of our city. The pathological isolationism bred by defacto segregation was challenged by the social explosions of the summers of 1966 and 1967. It woke many people up to the reality that the city had to become more inclusive in sharing the fruits of its labor with a greater sector of the population. The Urban Coalition was initially seen by many to hold the promise of being an effective instrument for a greater inclusion of justice and order in Minneapolis.

The business community was right to exercise leadership in drawing the city sectors of power and influence together under the umbrella of the Urban Coalition as it had become the most influential power community in the city. The minority communities saw the business community achieving a degree of social maturity. The business community commitment to lead in the creation of the Urban Coalition demonstrated a sense of responsibility to the other communities in the city.

For this reason the business community needs to be encouraged to continually invest its commitment to the Urban Coalition. It is important that the original covenant be kept. Should such a commitment soon fade, not given substance by daily acts of fidelity and forbearance through which lives are wedded and amalgamated, then the coalition will be an empty pledge. The Urban Coalition can become a key social experiment toward the integration of common interests in our city. The "our" has achieved a special significance since the summer of 1966. It means a city of haves and a city of have-nots, a house divided along economic and racial lines. This division within our own city must be seen with clarity as the Urban Coalition moves into making a covenant to rectify this house divided against itself.

The Urban Coalition must take on functions that face up to the new necessities of a city divided along racial and economic lines. On one hand, the Urban Coalition must be a bridge between the power communities represented by government, business, labor, schools, health community, religious groups, housing industry, and media.

The Urban Coalition can take its model from the United Nations. Simply stated, the UN Security Council would be the model for an executive council made up of power communities that would have permanent membership, along with rotating membership for various city neighborhoods. The UN General Assembly would be the model for the town forum where all neighborhoods and their groups, well defined by city history and name, would have a voice, as the smaller nations who have membership in the UN do, to discuss issues. As the city demographics change, so new neighborhoods and groups would be welcomed. The town forums or Assembly of Neighborhoods, as it could be called, can serve as a people's parliament. Here policies and sentiments of the people are submitted to the scrutiny of public opinion. In this public forum a particular group's interest must meet the test of its compatibility with the unity and order of the city.[27]

Anti-Racism Week and the Sensitivity Survey

Within a month, the Educational Task Force put a plan together and then sought to persuade the Urban Coalition to sponsor an Anti-Racism Week for the first week of May. Again, Louise McCannel was ahead of everyone as she worked out a plan for a week of conferences/workshops.[28] The Urban Coalition voted to sponsor a Racism Quotient Test, later renamed Sensitivity Survey, to be conducted throughout the metropolitan area during Anti-Racism Week. The religious community was the logical choice to take the survey as a significant share of the population gathered in synagogues and churches on a given weekend.

As a member of the Community Education Task Force, I became a committee of one to assemble the leaders of the Jewish and Christian religious bodies to secure their commitment to involve their congregations in the Anti-Racism Week. Van Konynenburg, president of Midwest Radio-Television, told me he would host the meeting at the Town House in the old WCCO building at LaSalle and Tenth Street. He would see that the religious leaders would be accompanied by the leaders of business who had started the Greater Minneapolis Urban Coalition.

As it turned out, all the religious leaders, save for the Southern Baptists who were new to Minnesota and the fledgling Islamic communities, were represented. We came together on Thursday, April 4—men of business and the men of religion, for they were all men in that room on that day, sitting and facing each other around a long table. Two power communities had come together for the first time to decide and to act jointly in a significant way to address a social ill that was jeopardizing lives for good, as well as undermining the good of the city.

The business leaders shared the Urban Coalition's plan for the Anti-Racism Week. The plan was straightforward. Ministers, priests, and rabbis, without prior announcement, would end their homily/sermon with a statement that the Urban Coalition had asked that on this Sabbath/Sunday all religious congregations in Minneapolis take the test, anonymously. A person, contacted by the coalition, would read a prepared statement and then administer the test. The tests would then be taken by that person to the regional racism quotient headquarters where a team of University of Minnesota social science students and a faculty member would compile the results. The racism quotient survey committee chair would then tabulate and interpret them. On the following Sabbath/Sunday, the survey results for the congregation would be discussed during the service.

The plan leading up to the sensitivity survey was then outlined to the religious leaders. The kick-off conference/workshop, locations for the week to be announced, was scheduled for the Monday preceding Anti-Racism Week with the theme "Do We Serve The Same Creator?" that would focus on religion's role in preventing the creation and perpetuation of racism in society. Then for each day of Anti-Racism Week there would be conferences/workshops for various groups. Monday, "How To Recognize Racism" for persons in mass communication media. Tuesday, "Housing Myths and Facts" for persons in housing and real estate business as well as community human rights groups. Wednesday, "How To Recruit Minority Employees" for business, labor, and industry. Thursday, "Racism Needn't Be Taught" for educators. Friday, "To Serve Us Equally" for local government agencies. Saturday, "Sound Health and Sound Recreation Eliminate Racism" for health and recreation leaders. Then during the following weekend services, the rabbis, priests, and preachers would have at it one last time as they share the significance of their particular congregation's test results. A Prejudice Quotient Test would be taken on a Twin Cities TV station by the general public on the Sunday ending Anti-Racism Week. It was a bold plan.

The religious leaders at the meeting agreed in principle but then began to hem and haw about the necessity to talk to subordinates. It was clear that such an approach would take weeks to go through ecclesiastical channels. I was chairing the meeting and with Van Konynenburg's support, along with nods from the business leaders, I said an executive decision needed to be made today by each of the religious leaders for the racism quotient test to be offered the first week in May. It was then that Bishop Kellogg took out his Episcopalian date book and planting it firmly on his Pickwickian stomach simply said, "What Sunday do you want?" It wasn't long before all the rest of the religious leaders had their date books out and a decision was made. Anti-Racism Week would become a reality.

Later that same day, the tragic news came that Dr. Martin Luther King, Jr. had been assassinated in Memphis. Moving forward with Anti-Racism Week became even more urgent. Immediately, Louise McCannel wrote a draft for Stephen Keating, as head of the Urban Coalition, to be mailed to various persons and groups inviting them to participate in one of Anti-Racism Week's conferences/workshops.

> Dr. Martin Luther King's assassination and the succeed-
> ing urban disturbances across the nation have again tragically
> illustrated the terrible consequences of the racism which per-

meates our culture. Efforts to relieve conditions in the ghettos and change White attitudes toward minorities must be accomplished by equally vigorous efforts to identify and treat the collective mental illness, which is racism. As a first step in that direction, the Greater Minneapolis Urban Coalition is undertaking an Anti-Racism Program to be launched with an Anti-Racism Mobilization Week.[29]

The plan was bold, too bold a learning curve for the Urban Coalition. There was trouble in Mill River City and it started with the computers. Those preparing the racism quotient test hit on technical snags involving such things as precise words and adequate pre-testing. However, the Sensitivity Survey, as it was now called, went forward as scheduled in early May, though technical problems would again delay the results for over six months. The day-long conference for religious leaders to discuss the implications of the survey was not conducted until the following December. The six-month delay was due to the tabulation of the results of the survey that had proved much more laborious and time consuming than originally anticipated. Out of the entire week plan of conferences/workshops only two were held.

The racial Sensitivity Survey, though the results long delayed, still provided revelatory material. Dr. Frank Wilderson, a Black sociologist on the faculty of the University of Minnesota, spoke regarding the methodology employed in the survey.

The Sensitivity Survey goes on a step further than any attitude inventories, questionnaires, and opinionaires that exist in the field today. In this survey the authors were concerned that the attitudes investigated be those that members of the Black community feel play a large part in the denial of equal access to opportunity to members of that group. It was, therefore, necessary that the survey not begin with the assumption that the attitudes of White America, which form barriers to progress of Black America, are well known. Rather the authors moved into the Black community and sought to gain from that community the impressions that Black people have of White racist attitudes, which bar Black progress. The

Sensitivity Survey, then, is an instrument that is designed to report the degree to which White church-goers hold attitudes, beliefs, and opinions that Black individuals feel have a negative or positive effect on Black progress.[30]

The *Tribune's* editorial headlines "Religion, Racism, and Paternalism" summed up the dominant attitude among White religious groups regarding race. The results of the survey came as a shock to many White Christians but was no surprise to African-American Christians. However the Black community was taken back by one observation.

> More than half the respondents did not feel that leaders in the cause of Black freedom must rest in the hands of Black men. Forty percent said that Black people are not in a position to understand fully the mechanics of getting changes made and thus need the direction of well-meaning White people. And a whopping 70 percent felt that Black people should realize that White people want to do what is in their best interest—the old "master knows best" syndrome.[31]

The editorial went on to challenge organized religion. The Sensitivity Survey will have been worthwhile if it brings a new awareness to White people of their attitudes on race. Awareness can be a big step toward change. It will have been doubly worthwhile if the churches now take up the challenge to educate their congregations to the Judaic-Christian teaching that all people are created equal, whatever their color. The editorial asked whether subsequent history would question whether the religious bodies and their leaders took up that challenge, indeed, if they had the wherewithal to carry forth such a conviction. If and where they did, it often came with a price.

Inner City Tensions Divides 60-Year-Old Congregation

Those words were the headlines for the *Minneapolis Star* Good Friday edition on March 27, 1970.[32] Calvary Methodist Church, predominantly a White congregation, had stood on the corner of Penn Avenue just two blocks south of Plymouth Avenue for nearly sixty years. Since the later fifties the congregation was finding it harder to attract new members from a changing inner city neighborhood. When I was appointed its pastor in the summer of 1965, I sought to change things around by having the congregation go out into the community rather than trying to get people into the church. This did bring new members who were attracted to a church that was seriously reaching out seeking to address the needs of people and community. The traditional members welcomed the new members but were uneasy about the turn in church life.

My identification particularly with **The Way** along with my affirmation with the emerging issues expressed in the empowerment of the poor and people of color helped to bring on a crisis that threatened to split the congregation.[33] The issue was brought to the Minnesota Annual Conference, the governing body of the Methodist Church meeting at Northfield, Minnesota, in June 1970.[34] The conference voted to establish and fund the new congregation that called itself the Peoples Church.[35] Many people left, leaving only a handful of persons to carry out a bold new ministry. Those few accomplished extraordinary things—creating an innovative day care center and a drug treatment program known as the Half Way Inn. I wrote about the drug program in the chapter "The Way and Ishmael." The church helped to create a day care center that was one of the first in the Twin Cities to utilize Black history and culture as its curriculum for preschool children.

I offered a tribute to those few known as the Peoples Church in these words spoken at my retirement adieu from the ministry. "In the inner city of death and new life, bold to sin and bolder by grace, I became my own preacher, faithful to myself. As a newborn bard of the Holy Spirit, I joined a small company of people who cast behind all conformity so we could acquaint men and women—at first hand—with Jesus. Always our most selves, God dwelt within."

A Civic Lesson in Power Yet To Be Learned

The work and cooperation that went into organizing Anti-Racism Week was one of the finer hours of the Greater Minneapolis Urban Coalition, a demonstration that showed various communities of power could come together, hear each other out, and make a mutual decision beneficial to the larger community. It was this initiatory power, so key to the early work of the Urban Coalition, that faded once leaders of various power communities abdicated their presence and, with it, the prestige of their direct support.

Jim Bowe, chairperson of the Community Education Task Force, resigned in protest against the emerging abdication of coalition leadership. I quote his letter at some length for it diagnosed the failure of the coalition to learn an important civic lesson.

> It is no secret to you that I have felt a growing dissatisfaction with the Coalition, stemming from increasing evidence that its operation has lost sight of its original concept.... Fundamentally, it seems to me that, rather than maintaining itself as a somewhat loose, open, and truly democratic forum, which welcomed all views and healthy challenge and argumentation, and in which an ordinary citizen could feel a sense of effective participation and response, the Coalition has become relatively closed, tightly structured, stratified, paternalistic and authoritarian....
>
> Another unhappy development has been the increasing apathy and disinterest both on the part of those who possess the power to effect real change and those who truly need and would benefit most by change.... This indifference, or alienation, was indicated most clearly only recently when a number of dissident board members requested me to arrange a meeting for them with some of the business leaders of the Coalition in order to discuss its operations, goals, and future. My attempt, through channels you established, was unsuccessful. The reason, I was told, was that "it had never been anticipated" that those business leaders would continue to be active in the affairs of the Coalition![36]

In any moral endeavor two requirements must be met. William James, a well known American psychologist, once defined the two requirements as: (1) resoluteness in the original commitment to the cause or discipline, and (2) a whole series of specific acts of loyalty to give historical body to the commitment.

The Greater Minneapolis Urban Coalition failed in its resolve to live up to its promise. It failed to fulfill William James' first requirement when leaders of the business community abdicated their role to various managers in their corporations. These representatives seldom spoke with authority and could never bind their corporation to any decisions that the coalition would make beyond the rudimentary objectives that characterized the coalition's work over the past several decades until its quiet demise.

The general malaise that has characterized the coalition in its latter years, disqualifying it as a effective instrument for social change, certainly relates to the second part of William James' requirement for moral action. The many years of continual commitment in small and large ways that speak of moral action, certainly required of the Greater Minneapolis Urban Coalition, did not evidence itself when the problems between the haves and have-nots could not be easily bridged. Without basic mutual trust no organizational system can help build community. One of the failings of the coalition was that it did not relate the power of business to the community of the poor. The power of business can be a resource for strength for the poor as well as it can prove a hazard. Power and weakness do not march easily in the same harness. It tempts the holders of power to pride as it tempts the weak to envy and resentment.

What happened to the Greater Minneapolis Urban Coalition was that the power brokers of business left breaking off significant dialogue between communities of power with people from various neighborhoods, many who saw themselves as disenfranchised. The business community was tempted to believe social problems could be solved like problems in business. That proved not to be the case. Responsibility for the city required a greater resolve than the leaders of business were ready to give to meet the ever evolving conflicting and competing desires of people from diverse backgrounds.

While the business community was tempted to resort to the security of its own business world, the communities of the disenfranchised faced another temptation. It came when social progress proved slow, tortuous, and sometimes contradictory. So many individuals and groups went their own way believing the coalition was just another organization that would finally make no difference for the poor and voiceless, many of whom to this day never even heard of the Greater Minneapolis Urban Coalition.

The coalition did begin with the high promise and commitment that sought to empower Minneapolis to become a co-operative city community. After four decades, the call to bring justice and order to the city is even more urgent, for Minneapolis is more divided by race and economics than ever before. This fact is made more tragic by the many so-called experts as they continue to entertain various theories intended to veil and obscure this tragic situation. No good purpose is served by minimizing the tragedy we are involved in. But no tragedy can serve any good purpose unless there is an instrument to achieve social justice. The Greater Minneapolis Urban Coalition failed not for being tried and found wanting; rather it was never wanted, so it was never tried.

Bringing Back an Equilibrium of Power

The city of Minneapolis is no different from other communities composed of a constellation of forces that precariously rests on the fulcrum of an equilibrium of power. Equilibrium is a necessity of government as it seeks to establish order, always curtailing what it regards as the inflated expense brought on by the demands of justice. Equilibrium is lost, the times out of joint, once justice is denied. Rulers misuse their power when they favor certain groups at the expense of others. Human society is an artful contrivance that enables people to serve one another even though their primary motive is to serve themselves.

Forty years ago a group of people came together from dissimilar backgrounds and understanding that had nothing in common but the strong conviction to create a voice to address inequity of power. Those people formed an organization and worked on its board and staff to make **The Way** a voice for people who lived their lives unheard, unseen, disregarded, and discarded. The need has not gone away. The challenge is even more urgent. It is not only a question of who will speak to power but how will such voices be heard and acted upon today.

SIX

ON MY WAY: COMING FULL CIRCLE

*The writing of this book has cast modesty aside
and shown me no other motive is needed
but to do the audacious.
I am no critic of the audacious,
simply a witness to its manifestations.*

—Rolland Robinson[1]

On My Way
From the Past to Our Future

The Way was born to keep alive the dream
that boldly believes
until all people are free
no one is truly free.

—Rolland Robinson[1]

Coming Back as for the First Time

At the beginning of this new millennium and new century, I returned
to the place where my life had undergone a transformation—the Near
North Side of Minneapolis. Coming back thirty-five years after I first
stepped foot in the community, I soon learned, even with the passage
of time, that it was much the same. It is a community bruised in its
soul, damaged by deceit, fantasy, and lame excuses. Why bother to
know the past when the present is so full of trouble? Harm comes to a
community that does not possesses a sense of its own history and so
lacks a critical way of thinking about itself. There is the understandable
reason dispossessed communities have little time for such things. Such
communities spend most of their waking hours dealing with the fall-
out that comes in fighting the shackles of poverty and racism as well as
its own personal demons. It can be said of the Near North Side of Minneapolis the struggle for human dignity and justice goes on; only the
faces have changed. This book cries out that this no longer be the way!

What I Hope to Leave Behind

There is a certain consternation that afflicts those, like myself, who seek to remember and, if it be known, seek to be remembered. I confess I have not always been forthright about such matters to you the reader, let alone to myself. I have hopes the struggle for freedom will carry on beyond myself, beyond **The Way**. Though I hold faintly to the suspicion, I have little right to insist on such audacious things. You can see how false modesty cripples me, standing in the way of writing boldly about myself and the good company I kept during certain conspicuous times in my life. The writing of this book has cast modesty aside and shown me no other motive is needed but to do the audacious. I am no critic of the audacious, simply a witness to its manifestations.

Me, an Upside Down We

I found myself writing a book I did not seek to write. There are other voices more articulate. I asked various witnesses over the years to write their remembrances of **The Way**, and they agreed that such a project was worthy and more–needed–but they did not write it. How does it happen that such tasks fall on those who have done most everything, or so they think, to avoid what has been given to them? Possibly, in this reluctance there is something more that needs to be said.

In the writing of this book I have discovered I was the one that needed to write it. I can now say of the confluence of words and narrative insights that unfolded through these pages, they came of their own accord, yet they came through me, through my point of view. Be assured, there are historical instances I have spoken of in this book, moments and insights to be prized, something to hold to, stories to be told to the next generation.

With some trepidation I came to write these concluding remarks about my own passage now come full circle. I thought a fitting coda would be what "we" have learned. But the royal "we" is too much for me to grasp if it meant embracing all those who were involved, touched, angered, or inspired by **The Way**. I certainly could not speak for them, though by innuendo that is what I have done. However, the royal "we" always meant you who in reading this book would join that splendid company to carry on the struggle of freedom. Why you? Because in these pages you have caught a glimpse of the horizon of your own possibilities; your upside down me has found its "we."

One never tells the young what they have yet to learn, for in youth's rare moment, it is sufficient they believe all things are possible. The prize worth keeping is that they never forget this moment no matter how much learning comes later. **The Way** was born when we were young. The young named **The Way**, and it was for them that it came into existence and had its being. It is for the young in spirit that this book is written so **The Way** will not be forgotten but reborn in a new way in and through them. We knew there was a difference, a passing, when **The Way** no longer felt itself young, worn down by the struggle, another horizon circling us, another youthful possibility being drawn beyond us—a newborning cry. For the moment we had **The Way**, believed we had found a treasure beyond price; for a moment, we believed all was possible, even the securing of a greater freedom for people who had long been engaged in its ancient struggle.

A Counter-Narrative that Would Make a Way

In the early days of **The Way**, a latter day rain of good fell upon us, falling on the just and unjust alike, seeping into every hole and pore of selfishness, not leaving any evil secure in its own satisfaction. That is what was powerful about **The Way. The Way** was not the last chapter of the struggle, yet it did give a glimpse to what the future would look like, a moment out of time, out of sync, a time without time commensurate to the work at hand. No mindful change can come, certainly not change in the evolutionary way, for the excellence we would turn into comes as others are bettered by the work we do. **The Way** holds its own lessons for its true successors.

If in the words of this book there is marked a course, not a blueprint but a passage, not the confines of a formula but an openness through a narrows where the imagination can make its liquid squeeze, breaking out of its shell, for the chrysalis to take flight, then those who come this way will know they are old before their time, yet also know how young they will again come to be. They will know that for a moment we had **The Way**.

SEVEN

Appendices

Appendix I
The Way Programs:
1966-1967

Project Big Sweep: 1967—Summer of Innovation

The Way's first summer was filled with the activity and excitement generated by Project Big Sweep. Like a large broom, the program was broad in scope sweeping through the community in areas that needed cleaning and attention. Community youth were given summer jobs on work crews assigned to clean up various parts of the Near North Side. Tot-Lots were run by high school and college students as job training classes were being offered for adults in various community churches.

The staff managed Project Big Sweep while **The Way** building was being renovated, and, in the midst of the chaos, the project began to take shape. Project Big Sweep was innovative as it involved seventy youth from the community to interact and work alongside college students. The Swahili word Harambee, meaning "together" or "let us pull together," came to designate the new spirit afoot personified by **The Way** in the summer of 1967.

Project Big Sweep was a litmus test for the programs the staff had been creating and developing with residents in response to the needs of the community over its first nine months. Three work areas were identified—Community Resources Exchange, Education Center, and Evening and Special Activities. Marcus Bell was named the program coordinator, a consultative position to Syl Davis, whose tasks were to evaluate programs and offer ways for improvement.

Community Resources Exchange

Community Resources Exchange's early efforts to reach out into the community were led by Willie Mae Dixon with the help of Eva Neubeck, Georgia O'Brien, and Joseph Gresham. Under Willie Mae's supervision, they conducted the community-training program that first summer. Staff and college students were trained how to conduct surveys that sought, through a series of non-directive questions, to identify the needs of the community. The staff encouraged persons to participate in various working community groups to seek some solution to existing problems.

The concept was straight forward—people working together to build community. Groups started with solvable problems like cleaning a block's back alley. The group organized block neighbors and, with the help of young people, cleaned the alley. Solving a small problem builds confidence to tackle bigger problems. This was **The Way** at its best, not dictating programs, but eliciting from persons ideas along with their wherewithal to solve their community problems. One of the fruits of this program was a Voter Registration Drive conducted the following summer. **The Way** coordinated the work of residents who went door to door. They registered nearly nine hundred persons for the 1968 fall elections.

Some Community Resources Exchange programs grew unexpectedly. Joseph Gresham began working for **The Way** in 1966. Soon he found himself helping people with the types of problems the poor and people of color experience—finding lawyers, getting to court, knowing one's rights. It was this kind of work that led to the creation of the Neighborhood Legal Complex and its involvement with the courts and corrections.

Another part of Community Resources Exchange included employment. Robert Love and Bill Wilson were in charge. Robert Love was a patient and caring man who worked tirelessly to provide job training and nearly single-handedly found jobs time and again for persons who were out of work. Bill Wilson came on staff as the manpower specialist to assist Robert Love in training and placement services, however budget restraints made it impossible for Bill Wilson to stay but a short time. Years later Bill Wilson was elected to St. Paul's City Council.

Bill Wilson saw **The Way** playing a key role in connecting with the very people that business and government agencies never saw. **The Way** was the right organization to do the job in offering job seminars. Seminars were designed to bring the applicant, who had been unemployed over a length of time or had no employment record, together with an employer. The initial classes taught persons how to conduct themselves in job interviews and how to write resumes when applying for a full-time job. The decision to employ or not to employ was made on the spot at **The Way.** If the employer gave reasons for not employing, then the leaders of the seminar took this into account toward helping the person with the next interview.

Education Center

Project Big Sweep's education program was divided into the areas of Basic Skills and Minority History. Teachers came forward to contribute their time. Marcus Bell, a teacher in the Minneapolis School System, taught basic reading, writing, and arithmetic classes. That same summer Robert Williams, a counselor at Lincoln Learning Center, came to aid in the administration and scoring of the basic skills tests. The special attention given to these children helped many to improve their basic skills and so encouraged them to remain in school. This program later became **The Way Laboratory School** under the direction of Gwyn Jones-Davis.

Minority history classes were taught by Mahmoud El-Kati. These classes offered persons of color as well as White persons insight into African-American cultural heritage. Social problems were believed to be often the result of ignorance that led to misunderstanding. Knowledge would help a person break free from ignorance fed on racist ideas and attitudes by offering tools for community building. The **University of The Way** grew out of these classes and offered courses on Black studies with the intent to prepare persons for college.

Evening and Other Activities:
The Arts of Self Defense and Self-Expression

The Evening and Other Activities was **The Way's** recreation program that reached out to young people after school and on weekends. This was managed by Frank Jackson who worked with Dan Pothier, the Institutional Coordinator. Dan, who developed the Black Patrol in the summer of 1967, worked closely with Harry "Spike" Moss who directed the youth program. Other part-time recreational workers included Wade Russell, Sumner Jones, Gary "Mousey" Paterson, Michael Reese, and Michael Crawford. Charles Harris was the boxing instructor who taught the ancient art to aspiring pugilists.

The evening program worked on the basis that youth best related to other youth. Soon a group emerged known as the Taschaka Zulu Warriors, and, under the direction of Spike Moss, held their own rap sessions. The rap sessions were conducted by five post-high school persons known as the Black Guard. Black young men who had confronted their problems were now trying to help younger brothers to get real about the world and its dangers of dope and alcohol before it turned them into hustlers and thieves.

The arts program was one of those activities that grew unexpectedly. Interest in the arts forced the program to search for new space. In the fall of 1967 a vacant store building at 1905 Plymouth Avenue, next door to **The Way**, was used to house plays, workshops, and studio space for artists and dancers. Karamu in Swahili means "gathering place for festivities." Karamu was the name of the arts program that centered itself in theater, dance, art, and music under the direction of artist Robert Banner. Persons from the art world, such as the Guthrie Theater, came as volunteers to offer classes and some to direct plays such as *Trial of Brother Jero* and *Clara's Ole Man* along with one act plays by the Nigerian playwright Wole Soinka. The intensive schedule can be seen in one week's offering of classes that included creative and play writing, speech workshops, theater improvisation and mime, ethnic dance, drawing classes, and jazz and public performances on weekends. It became a training ground for developing artists. Endesha Holland, who was known as Aida Mae Holland when she worked at **The Way**, later went on to become a playwright with *Mississippi Dela* to her credit.

A building on Portland Avenue was found in 1967 to run a youth program in South Minneapolis under the leadership of Ronald Welsh, a former Catholic priest. It also housed **The Way** newspaper published by Vusmusi Zulu and Josephine "Togo" Willis. The paper's first issue was published in August 1968, and visually declared itself in the horrific picture of a dead Black man. His smoldering body lay prostrate on the dying embers of a fire that lit the White faces of grinning men. **The Way** newspaper's printed its own manifesto.

> This paper is the direct result of a gross need within our community. It aims to inform and make aware all elements within our community (i.e., Blacks, Negroes, Whites, of all standings and others) who are at present without the power of definition and consequently unable to effectively deal with the crisis of the fascistic posture of this nation. We would hasten to add that "newspaper" is perhaps not an accurate description of these pages. We intend more than just that. We are by our very existence an indictment of the existing news media. All and each of them—whether it be radio, TV, newspapers, or the Negro press—have failed miserably in their duty of relating, defining, and articulating those things which affect each of our everyday lives. We pledge not to become a vehicle for personal vendettas for personal gain; nevertheless, no injustice or conspiracy to violate human rights will escape our scathing attention. In short, we accept that which all others have either failed or refused to accept. We must not fail. For to fail in projection of what is—rather than what should or could be—is to become so hypnotized by the graceful movements of the cobra that we become his prey. We, therefore, dedicate these pages to ourselves, the Black community, for our survival as a people rather than as tools.[1]

The paper always got a strong response. One particular board meeting erupted into condemnations as Jewish board members said they were offended by the newspaper's use of anti-Semitic stereotypes and cliches.[2] **The Way** newspaper didn't back off, but some of the board members did by leaving the board.

Day at The Way

People continued to come to see for themselves just what **The Way** was all about. The first person a visitor would meet would be Henrietta Adams, or Eunice Pierro, or Verlena Matey-Keke. This trio were the receptionists when they were not providing secretarial support for Syl Davis and the program staff. They were the first persons one met when coming into the building. Some persons tried these sisters' patience yet their wit was always ready to answer difficult questions. The receptionist on duty was often successful in getting people through the front door and, more often than not, taking them on tour of the building, sharing the excitement in the activity that was going on at **The Way.** The job often involved late hours. Verlena Matey-Keke was on duty in the early morning hours of August 13, 1969 when the police rushed people on Plymouth Avenue, forcing them into **The Way** for safety. [read **The Way** and Media]

Nothing was constant at **The Way**, save controversy. All things were in flux, save fighting for justice. Such was the chaos and creativity and motive that went with the place and that the staff, to their credit, worked with day after day. Such was a day at **The Way.**

Appendix II
The Way Programs:
1968-1970

We Are Building the Way:
Developing Effective Models of Community Reform

By 1968, **The Way** formed a research and education effort devoted to creating social vehicles of reform and redevelopment. The first years (1966-1967) were seen as experimentation in organizing the community. **The Way** worked with a wide array of North Side residents in training and practical planning. The staff decided it was now ready to engage people in developing and demonstrating a comprehensive approach to community reform.

The Way had begun to learn what other Black groups were doing in other parts of the country. Some members of **The Way** staff took it upon themselves to contact various Black organizations in other cities as they visited kinfolk. They brought back information of what they had witnessed. The next step was to send staff to investigate well-known Black community organizing efforts in various parts of the country. Harry "Spike" Moss and Gwyn Jones-Davis traveled to different cities to investigate the models and methods of different types of community organizations. Spike's trip was sponsored by OEO [Office of Economic Opportunities] as Gwyn received support from Youth Organizations United. On their return Gwyn and Spike worked with staff and me in developing a set of guidelines for effective community organization. I had traveled to Chicago to check out the Ecumenical Institute organizing effort known as Fifth City. The result of our work is described below.

Evaluation Model

The first task in community organization is developing criteria for judging the effectiveness of existing efforts. Five guidelines were developed to measure current community organizations and urban programs.

1. *Democratic Guideline:* Key to any community effort is the degree of participation relative to the population of the community. No group, however large in number, however financially powerful, however wisely informed, can force a model upon a community. Such a structure may be accepted externally, but the people in the community will not have assumed responsibility for it. The effectiveness of the organizing agency is measured by the degree it involves the people of the community in developing and assuming responsibility for their own model of community organization.

2. *Universal Guideline:* The effectiveness of any community effort is relative to the development of an ever widening sense of responsibility on the part of its participants. This can be visualized as a series of circles, the smallest being the self, the next the family or extended family, next the neighborhood, and outward to the ward, the city, the metropolitan area, and beyond to the world. Immediate self-interest may provide much of the basis for initial organizing [Project Big Sweep demonstrated how self interest is used to involve people. Read appendix I "The Way Programs: 1966-1967."] However, unless the circle of responsibility is enlarged, the organization will parochially turn in on itself and contribute to the problems of the community rather than being part of the solution. [An example is groups formed in opposition to other groups. Read, "The Way People Can Speak to Power."]

3. *Pragmatic Guideline:* The effectiveness of any organizing effort is relative to the degree of practical success it has in solving the concrete problems of the community. [Project Big Sweep organizing efforts in cleaning back alleys is an example of practical organization.] It is legitimate to ask to what degree economic dependency

has been reduced or political participation increased [**The Way's** Voter Registration Drive registered nearly nine hundred voters] or illiteracy eliminated. [Project D.A.R.E. found ways to reach and teach young people who had dropped out of public school. Read "The Way Toward Inclusive Education."]

4. *Individual Guideline:* The effectiveness of any community effort is judged in part by the personal growth of the individuals who participate in it. A successful community project should show evidence of people who have become more self-reliant and more able to cope with everyday problems on their own. [**The Way's** employment seminars offered the necessary encouragement for persons who had been out of work for long periods of time in showing how to conduct themselves in job interviews. Read appendix I "The Way Programs: 1966-1967."]

5. *Durability Guideline:* The effectiveness of community organization is its ability to deal not only with immediate crises but to sustain long range efforts demanded in working at the root causes of community problems.[1] [The entire effort at community organization was abandoned by the administration of **The New Way.**]

Previous Models

The Way staff and I, using our evaluation model, then evaluated three approaches to community redevelopment.

1. *Government Sponsored Approach:* This approach has gone under the label of urban renewal. The strength of this approach is the availability of money and support of powerful urban leaders to ensure implementation. The weakness in these efforts is they have token participation on the part of community residents. Participants were generally found to be persons who were responsible to the urban power leadership and not to the constituency of the community. These efforts were often not in the self-interest of the community residents but were aimed at relocating residents in other geographical areas. In their place came more affluent residents or businesses along with industrial developments that benefit particular persons or groups with power and influence. [The Glenwood-Lyndale Redevelopment Plan proved how disastrous such government sponsored programs can be for

a community and its residents. Read "The Way Toward Renewal of Public Life."] H. Wentworth Eldredge described the failure of this approach in his book *Taming Megalopolis* written over forty years ago.

2. *Problem Orientated Approach:* Religious organizations and various service agencies follow this approach. The gift of this approach is that it meets immediate and pressing needs of persons usually on an individual basis. However, such groups lack the resources to meet the needs of people over a long period of time. This approach tends to perpetuate the cycle of dependency and self depreciation. Several years ago, Charles E. Silberman stated, in his work *Crisis in Black and White*, that such problem-orientated groups see, as their goal, the treatment of individuals who are maladjusted. He insisted their goal be enlarged toward making social changes to relieve the forces that circumscribe the lives of people.

3. *Grass Roots Community Organization:* Grass roots organization has the value of involving people in defining problems, setting goals, and implementing programs. The gift of this approach is that it encourages self-determination and dignity by guaranteeing that at least some of the problems dealt with will be issues of priority for the community. The downside is that there is a high mortality rate with such organizations. One of the more durable and significant approaches in organizing communities is by bringing together, under a one-umbrella organization, many different organizations such as business, religious institutions, social service agencies, labor, education, the media etc. [The Urban Coalition was an example of this type of umbrella organization. The causes of its demise are discussed in "The Way People Can Speak To Power."] The community organization method often fails to yield the results demanded by the evaluation guidelines stated above. The organization may cover an entire city of hundreds of thousands of people yet only involves a few that usually end up to be paid staff after the charismatic personalities have disappeared. The self-interest of participating groups in such organizations may war against the use of necessary power to bring about social change for oppressed communities.[2]

Developing a New Model
for Community Redevelopment

After considering the existing efforts at community organization, **The Way** staff developed a model of community redevelopment designed to meet the evaluation guidelines it had set for itself. This was stated in five organizing methods.

1. *A Defined Geo-Social Area:* Community identity is key to community organization. By clearly defining the area, a community identity can be used to promote solidarity and affords the maximum participation by residents. Kevin Lynch, in his book *The Image of the City*, developed the model for a geo-social map that we are using. Boundaries of the Near North Side were the natural boundary of the Mississippi River to the east, the political boundary of the city limits to the west. The dominant roadways of Olson Highway to the south and Broadway to the north defined the other two edges of the community. Other paths were thoroughfares that ran north and south such as Penn and Lyndale Avenues. Plymouth Avenue was the main path through the heart of the community and was a center of community activity and meeting places [**The Way**; Urban League, then a small storefront located further east on Plymouth Avenue; Dr. Thomas Johnson's clinic; and Reverend Orpheus Williams' store front church] as Broadway Avenue served as the shopping hub.

2. *Defining the Depth Human Problem of the Community:* Comprehensive community reform is to discern and attack the depth human problem of the community. Responsible participation and lasting results are dependent upon the degree the root problem is addressed and solved. Contemporary psychology and sociology have revealed that the way a human being images oneself in their situation is key to their effectiveness in solving problems. If a person imagines oneself as a inner city resident who is a victim of circumstances, that person will not be responsive to efforts to involve him or her in effective community reform. The challenge is to have the negative self-image replaced with one of significance. Then one becomes capable of changing the shape of their life and of their community.

3. *All Community Problems Attacked Simultaneously:* A comprehensive and coordinated effort is key to effective social change. The solution of any particular problem is related to the solution of every other problem. The natural scientist and the urban sociologist have taught the interrelationship of all things. We can see how the problems of unemployment reinforce the problem of housing, and the problems of education and health reinforce the problem of unemployment. To attack only one problem is a losing battle. Every area of social existence—*cultural, political,* and *economic* must be dealt with in a comprehensive and coordinated fashion if lasting solutions are to be achieved.

4. *Deal With All Age Levels At Once:* The child continually appropriates the images of the adult world while adults are often changed by the rebellion of their children. If the problems of the aged are not met, the solutions to the problems of every other age group are undercut both by the influence of the aged and the awareness that every younger generation has its own destiny to become elders themselves. If the problems of children are not met, it only ensures the future adult generation will perpetuate the same social problems. If the problems of the middle aged are not met, then their problems will continue to manifest themselves in the older and younger generations. If a community organization is to be effective in involving people in reshaping their community, in solving their problems, and in ministering to individual needs, then programs and structures that involve all age groups are required.

5. *Use Of Symbols:* Groups have always marched behind banners that declare their identities. Marcus Garvey's Universal Negro Improvement Association during the 1920s demonstrated in their dress and literature the power of symbols of Black nationalism. This is equally true for community groups that need to create symbols that express their identity. If the depth problem is the key to effective community reform, then the use of symbols is the key to the solution to the depth problem. The self image of a person is changed when one has a new set of symbols that holds new possibilities for one's actions. Symbols may rise out of myth and folk tales of people that empower one to see oneself as a member of a

significant community. Symbols are needed that have the power to provide a sense of unity in purpose and action necessary for effective community reform. [**The Way** logo (We, an upside down Me) was developed as a symbol for community building.][3]

The Way's Model for Developing and Demonstrating A Comprehensive Approach to Community Reform

KARAMU

Establishing Cultural Identity

> **Responsibility:** To sustain humanness in the city through the celebration of the constants of life: birth, death, struggle, and change.

> **Karamu:** Develop effective corporate symbolic structures to deal with the problems of:

> 1. *Human Dignity:* The inner city problems relating to the wide spread of racist images that paralyze persons of color.

> 2. *Inner City Significance:* Inner city problems relating to the creative role of the community in creating new images of itself.

> 3. *Global Community:* Inner city problems relating to the needs of the poor and the oppressed in every country and to act in solidarity with them.

> **Karamu:** These are the structures that bring solutions.

> 1. **The Way** *Players:* The art of the theater offers a sense of community and celebration of culture.

> 2. **The Way** *Ensemble:* The body and the voice are gifts that need to be channeled into various cultural expressions. The ensemble does this through its dance and music groups.

> 3. **The Way** *Artistry:* The visual arts (painting, sculpture) offer the opportunity for individual expression of one's heritage.

> 4. *The People's Festival:* Cultural celebrations are necessary forms in building unity.

HARAMBEE

Reorganizing Community Relationships

Responsibility: To provide creative involvement in shaping the life styles of urban society, including the manners, dress, neighborhood, and sociability that makes life meaningful.

Harambee: Develop effective community structures for various life styles to deal with the problems of:

1. *Established Generation:* Inner city problems relating to the breakdown of family and neighborhood ties.

2. *Emerging Generation:* Inner city problems relating to the need of youth culture for creating structures in the development of their possibilities.

3. *Rising Generation:* Inner city problems relating to the absence of social forms geared to the expansion of the lives of the younger youth.

4. *Elder Generation:* Inner city problems relating to the sense of insignificance among the elderly resulting from the lack of social involvement forms.

Harambee: These are the structures that bring solutions.

1. *Tschaka Zulu Warriors:* The thrust of the group is to provide the safe place for young black men to begin to pull themselves together. This group carries the responsibility for the creation of new leaders.

2. **The Way** *Project—Leadership and Management:* An intense learning course for young men and women in ways to handle their lives with poise and maturity.

3. **The Way** *Project—D.A.R.E.:* "Development of the Abilities of Rejected Egos" is a cooperative educational experience with the correctional institutions in working with paroled persons.

4. **The Way** *Project—S.P.U.R.:* "Stimuli Project Upward Reaches" is designed to work directly with staffs at correctional institutions through the use of African-American consultants.

5. **The Way** *Rehabilitative Center:* A safe place where people of the inner city can come together in the life-giving atmosphere of a woodland camp setting. There they learn to give and live with each other in an environment of mutual support.

UNIVERSITY OF THE WAY

Increasing Education Capabilities

Responsibility: To train and educate the imagination of the people so they are equipped to build new urban structures.

University Of The Way: Develop effective community structures to deal with the problems of:

1. *Public Schooling:* Inner city problems relating to subnormal conditions in public schools that prevent the creative growth of youth.

2. *Adult Education:* Inner city problems relating to the need for adult training essential to providing strong community leadership.

3. *Supplementary Training:* Inner city problems relating to the need of children for intensive early education and the lack of institutions to advance learning.

4. *Advanced Preparation:* Inner city problems relating to bridging the gap between the inner city and institutions of advanced learning.

University Of The Way: These are the structures that bring solutions.

1. **The Way** *Project—Chain Gang*: In cooperation with the public schools, **The Way** offers various courses for credit for high school dropouts.

2. **The Way** *Education Center*: Classes on African-American culture are offered by **The Way** to restore the gift of heritage and the strength it provides.

3. **The Way** *Day Care Center:* The center provides child care for working parents as well as offering classes in child-raising for young parents.

4. **The Way** *Laboratory School:* The school provides alternative learning strategies for grade school students who have been alienated from the public school system.

URBAN ENABLEMENT ORGANIZATION

Building Indigenous Leadership

Responsibility: To order community life and enable the people to make corporate decisions about the future of their community.

Urban Enablement Organization: Develop effective community political structures to deal with the problems of:

1. *Fundament Order:* Inner city problems relating to the basic peace and order required by any community for the well-being of its citizens.

2. *Human Rights:* Inner city problems relating to the tragic ignorance of basic rights and absence of adequate structures to protect and insure those rights.

3. *Effective Suffrage:* Inner city problems relating to forces that prohibit the poor and persons of color from participating in the decisions that determine their lives.

4. *Urban Services:* Inner city problems relating to flagrant inequities in providing everyday services that urban life requires.

Urban Enablement Organization: These are the structures that give solutions.

1. **The Way** *Soul Force and Black Patrol:* These groups have insured the safety of the inner city and so secured peace and order for the community.

2. **The Way** *Legal Service:* This service provides the liaison between police, courts, prisons with community residents who have difficulty in finding their way through the legal and penal system.

3. **The Way** *Project—Voter Registration:* The organization of community residents to register their neighbors to vote

overcame the difficulties many faced in going downtown to city hall to register.

4. **The Way** *Community Services:* Organizing residents to see that snow removal, garbage collection, paving of streets, and other city services were provided as promised.

URBAN SERVICES EXCHANGE

Developing Community Resources

Responsibility: To nurture the health and security of residents so that they may creatively contribute to the good life they have a right to share in.

Urban Services Exchange: To develop effective community economic structures to deal with the problems of:

1. *Competent Income:* Inner city problems relating to human deterioration and disruption through inadequate and irregular income.

2. *Consumer Protection:* Inner city problems relating to the vicious exploitation of the poor and persons of color in the exchange of goods.

3. *Adequate Housing:* Inner city problems relating to the rapid deterioration of housing in the inner ring communities that surround downtown.

4. *Health Security:* Inner city problems relating to the limited resources and know how that ensures maintenance of basic health.

Urban Services Exchange: These are the structures that provide solutions.

1. **The Way** *Employment Service:* **The Way** works with persons who find little help from employment agencies in securing jobs. Seminars are conducted to provide persons with skills and confidence for job interviews. Arrangements are made to have potential employers come to **The Way** to interview applicants.

2. **The Way** *Project—Housing:* **The Way** advocates for community residents in securing adequate housing for their

families. **The Way** works with other advocacy groups to secure tenants' rights and code enforcement.

3. **The Way** *Project—Support Black Doctors:* **The Way** works with Black doctors in the community in recruiting Black physicians and in securing financial resources in upgrading their medical and health services.[4]

The Way is Open to You

What has not been included in this appendix is the extensive work that had been done by **The Way**, nor are the plans of implementation included. Should you be interested in investigating further you can research **The Way** documents in the Minnesota Historical Society.

You can sense the breadth and depth of vision **The Way** brought to the task of community redevelopment. It is this vision and the will to carry it forth that need to be carried on by a new generation of pragmatic visionaries.

Appendix III
Brief History Of The Way

Chronicle of Events

1966

August   Plymouth Avenue street violence.

Meeting in North Side park with Governor Rolvag and Mayor Naftalin.

Ray Plank leads the business community in finding jobs.

1913 Plymouth Avenue building opens and is run by volunteer staff offering job placement and recreation.

The Way is given its name by young people.

The Way board of directors is organized. Dr. Gerald Lee named president. Syl Davis named director.

September   Volunteer staff canvasses community by talking to residents to determine community needs.

Work commissions established.

Articles of Incorporation drafted.

Development of plans for remodeling 1913 building.

$24,000 raised in first month.

The Way staff receives first paychecks.

December $32,000 raised for remodeling building.

$4,146 paid to staff for 1966.

$64,025 operating budget for 1967.

Meeting on North Side with Governor-elect Harold LeVander.

1967

January   **The Way** board receives the work commission's first-progress reports. Commission reports include Religious Unity, Employment, Youth Action, Education, and Law Enforcement.

The first brochure on **The Way** is printed.

February   Articles of Incorporation and By-laws governing the board and organization adopted.

March   New board officers elected. Rolland Robinson named new president.

June   Project Big Sweep begins.

Employment Seminars offered.

Summer '67 jobs program.

D.A.R.E., S.P.U.R..

Heritage and Leadership classes.

Fund raising: $107,000 raised since August 1966.

Work begins on remodeling the building at a cost of $93,000. $45,000 raised to date.

Additional funds to be pledged.

South Side Way opens and board appoints supervisory committee.

July   Second street violence on Plymouth Avenue.

National Guard called out by governor.

Black Patrol organized by Dan Pothier.

Louise McCannel calls a meeting of fifteen business leaders that will become the nucleus of the Greater Minneapolis Urban Coalition.

August Grand jury begins its investigation into the causes of the riot.

September Grand jury report made public. No criminal charges are made, yet **The Way** is criticized.

December Lincoln Junior High school slapping incident: A White teacher slaps a Black Student.

The Way negotiates with school officials as a school boycott is called by a community group that closes the school before Christmas break.

1968

February Formation of the Greater Minneapolis Urban Coalition.

March Civil Liberties Union publicly criticizes the grand jury report on **The Way**.

April Dr. Martin Luther King, Jr. assassinated.

March of Support passes **The Way** and is stopped by police claiming snipers were on the roof of **The Way**. Rumor proved false. March moves on to Calvary Methodist Church to organize human rights groups in White neighborhoods through-out the Twin Cities.

Greater Minneapolis Urban Coalition goes ahead with plans for Anti-Racism Week and conducting "Racial Profile Survey" in Greater Minneapolis religious communities.

Soul Force, started at **The Way,** becomes a city-wide effort under the sponsorship of the Urban Coalition.

June Harambe programs incorporated: Tschaka Zulu Warriors, D.A.R.E., S.P.U.R.

July University of The Way incorporated: Laboratory School, Operation Chain Gang, Education Center, Day Care Center.

September   Urban Enablement Programs incorporated: Neighborhood Legal Complex, Voter Registration.

Karmau incorporated: Art programs move in next door to **The Way** building at 1905 Plymouth Avenue.

Urban Services Programs incorporated: Employment Services, Work with Tenant Rights groups, Support for Black Doctors.

December   **The Way** is featured in *Minneapolis Tribune's* "Picture Magazine."

Results of the "Racial Profile Survey" are released.

1969

April   **The Way** supports three Black students indicted by the grand jury for protesting at the University of Minnesota.

August   Two nights of police confrontations with residents on Plymouth Avenue.

October   Initial report of comprehensive community organization programs to the board.

1970

January   **The Way's** Model for Developing a Comprehensive Approach to Community Reform is unveiled.

May   Syl Davis is arrested on drug charge in St. Louis, Missouri.

October   Syl Davis announces his resignation as director.

November   Bert Davis is named interim director of **The New Way**

December   Syl Davis is cleared of drug charges.

1971

January Rolland Robinson resigns as president of the board.

Reverend Merle Carlson elected president.

Bert Davis becomes the director.

June **University of The Way** becomes **Antioch-Minneapolis Communiversity.**

December **The New Way** is approved as a United Way agency.

1973

December Louise McCannel resigns from the board.

1974

January Harry "Spike" Moss becomes **The New Way** director.

1979

June **Antioch-Minneapolis Communiversity** graduates last class.

1982

January Syl Davis becomes the president of the board.

1984

May Syl Davis resigns as president. Hobart Mitchell, Jr. named new president.

December **The New Way's** building is completed. The new building cannot be used as the United Way cuts program funds.

1989

A North Side community group, led by Verlena Matey-Keke, reorganizes **The Way** board and seek to reclaim the building. The matter is taken to court. The group is not given the building. The City, a United Way agency, takes over the building.

Notes

Dedication

1. Thoreau, Henry David, quoted by Mahmoud El-Kati, "*A Tribute to Syl Davis*" at Zion Baptist Church (7 April 1992), The Way Documents, Minnesota Historical Society. Quotes are taken from *Walden, Conclusion,* (New York: Bantum Classics, 1965), pp. 344, 346.

Preface

1. McCannel, Louise, Correspondence, (4 December 1967), The Way Documents, Minnesota Historical Society.

ONE: Author's Introduction

1. Robinson, Rolland, Speech Delivered at Minnesota Annual Conference of The United Methodist Church, (1 June 2000), Author's documents.

A Way Of Writing

1. Frost, Robert, "Provide, Provide", quoted by Randall Jarrell, *Poetry and the Age*, (New York: Alfred A. Knopt, 1955), p. 40.

2. Thurman, Howard, *Jesus and The Disinherited*, (Nashville: Abington-Cokesbury, 1949), p. 60.

3. Said, Edward, *Reflections on Exile,* quoting Theodore Adorno, (Cambridge: Harvard University Press, 2000), pp. 263-264.

Taking A Read On The Way

1. *North Side Memories*, Phil Freshamn and Linda Mack Schloff editors, Jewish Historical Society of the Upper Midwest, (2002).

The Way Of Telling The Story Right: The Unlikeliness Of A Documentary Or Leaving Sociology To The Scientists

1. Ellison, Ralph, *Shadow & Act*, (New York: Signet Books, 1966), p. 113.
2. Metro-Poll, (9 April 1968), *Minneapolis Star*.

TWO: Part Biography, Part Fiction

1. Ackroyd, Peter, (10 January 1999), *New York Times Book Review*.

Syl Davis

1. Davis, Syl, Author's Documents, 1966-2006.
2. Psalm 24:5, Revised Standard Version.
3. Davis, Syl, (1996-2006), op. cit.
4. Ibid.
5. Ibid.

Willie Mae Dixon

1. Gospel of John 8:32, Revised Standard Version.

THREE: A Nearly Forgotten History

1. Auden, W.H. and Louis Kronenberger, *The Viking Book of Aphorisms*, (New York: Viking Press, 1962), p. 239.

Part One: Trying To Find The Way

1. Taylor, David, "Much Local Black History Lost," (3 February 2005), *Spokesman-Recorder*.

Part Two: It Couldn't Happen Here

1. Davis, Syl, "In The Beginning," (17 August 1968, Vol. 1, No. 1 *The Way Newspaper*), The Way documents, Minnesota Historical Society.

Part Three: How The Way Got Its Name

1. Ibid.

Part Four: The Grand Jury Report On The Way

1. "The Grand Jury Racial Riot Report," (13 September 1967), *Minneapolis Tribune*.
2. "The Way Deserves a Chance to Succeed," (17 October 1967), *Minneapolis Tribune*.
3. Hennepin County Grand Jury Report, (12 September 1967), The Way documents, Minnesota Historical Society.
4. Grow, Doug, "Naftalin Didn't Understand How Good He Was," (19 May 2005), *Minneapolis Star Tribune*.

5. Minnesota Civil Liberties Union Board of directors, (May 1968) The Way documents, Minnesota Historical Society.

6. The Way Board of directors, (March 1968), The Way documents, Minnesota Historical Society.

7. Minnesota Civil Liberties Union Board of directors, (May 1968), op.cit.

8. Ibid.

9. The Way Board of directors, (April 1969), The Way documents, Minnesota Historical Society.

Part Five: The Way For Its Time

1. Davis, Syl, Author's documents (1966-2006).

2. El-Kati, Mahmoud, "A Tribute to Syl Davis," (1992), Author's documents.

3. El-Kati, Mahmoud, Historical Statement for Seventeenth Annual Board of Directors, (1984), Author's documents.

4. El-Kati, Author's documents (1966-2006).

5. Greenwald-Davis, Barbara, (March 1998) conversation with author.

6. "Observers Say The Way Didn't Make Changes Needed To Keep Funding," (10 December 1984), *Minneapolis Tribune.*

FOUR: The Way of Struggle

1. Douglas, Frederick, *Address to Colored People*, (1848), Author's documents.

The Way and Ishmael The Street Brother

1. "Manchild Twenty Years Later," (15 October 1984), *Minneapolis Tribune.*

2. Hennepin County Grand Jury Report, (May 1968), op. cit.

3. Syl Davis interviewed by Gerald Vizenor, (October 1967), *Twin Citian*, pp. 60-62.

4. Fanon, Frantz, *Black Skins White Masks,* (New York: Grove Press, 1967), p. 215.

5. Ibid. p. 220, note 8.

6. Ellison, Ralph, *Invisible Man*, (New York: Signet Books, 1952). p. 8.

7. Epistle to Galatians 4:21-26, Revised Standard Version.

8. Book of Genesis 16:2, Revised Standard Version.

9. Spaulding, James, Letter, (19 April 1972), Author's documents (1966-2005)

The Way and the Law

1. Auden and Kronenberger, *op. cit.,* p. 208.
2. "Jordan Near Riot," (23 August 2002), *Minneapolis Star Tribune.*
3. Samuels, Don, (September 2002), "Salvaging, Don't Savage Jordan Neighborhood," *Minneapolis Star Tribune.*
4. Pothier, Dan, phone conversation with author, (August 2002).
5. Ahmed, A. Karim, (February 1969), "Side By Side On The North Side," *Ivory Tower*, University of Minnesota, Minnesota Historical Society.
6. Burke, Kenneth, *Terms of Order*, (Bloomington: Indiana University Press, 1964), p. 130.
7. Baldwin, James, *Esquire* (July 1968).
8. Neighborhood Legal Complex program proposal, (1968), **The Way** documents, Minnesota Historical Society.
9. Dubois, Dr. W.E.B. *The Souls of Black Folk*, (Greenwich, Connecticut: Fawcett Publication, Inc., 1961), pp. 16-17.
10. Magee, Dr. Robin, Faculty of Hamline University, Presentation at Conference on Racial Reconciliation, Hennepin Avenue United Methodist Church, (5 April 2003).

The Way and Minneapolis

1. Ellul, Jacque, *The Meaning of the City,* (Grand Rapids: Eerdmans, 1970).
2. Coleman, Nick, (5 September 2004), "Revisionists Replace History With Hostility," *Minneapolis Star Tribune.* "Taxpayers League sought to change Olson Highway to the Ronald Regan Highway."
3. Auden, W.H., quoted by Burke, Kenneth, *Rhetoric of Religion*, (Boston: Beacon Press, 1961), *p. 4-5.*
4. Campbell, Joseph, *Masks of God: Occidental Mythology*, (New York: Viking Press, 1970), pp. 313-317.
5. Book of Genesis 4:9-17, Revised Standard Version.
6. Ibid. 1:28.
7. Szarkowski, John, *The Face of Minnesota*, (Minneapolis: University of Minnesota Press, 1958), p. 3.
8. Ellul, Jacque, *The Meaning of the City*, op. cit., pp. 9-10.
9. Epistle of Colossians 1:16, Revised Standard Version.
10. Wink, Walter, *Naming the Powers*, (Philadelphia: Fortress Press,1984), pp. 64-67.
11. Book of Genesis 11:4, Revised Standard Version.
12. Forbes, James, (February 2002) Author's notes from address given at Augsburg College, Author's documents.

13. Book of Isaiah 2:4, Revised Standard Version.

14. Gospel of Luke 19:42, Revised Standard Version.

15. Gospel of Luke 13:34, Revised Standard Version.

The Way and the Media

1. Auden, W.H., quoted *The Dyer's Hand*, (New York: Vintage Press, 1968), p. 93.

2. Murray, Albert, *The Omni Americans*, (New York: Da Capo Press, 1970), p. 103.

3. Ivins, Molly, "Profile Of Confrontation: How It Was on North Side," (24 August 1969), *Minneapolis Tribune*.

4. "OEO Turns Anti-Agitator," (21 September 1969), *Minneapolis Star*.

5. Vusmusi, Zulu, (10 May 1999), *Insight News*, Author's documents.

6. The Way Board of directors, (May 1970), The Way documents, Minnesota Historical Society.

7. Ibid.

8. Alsop, Frank, (10 October 1970), *Minneapolis Tribune*.

9. Pillow, Edgar D., Ibid.

10. Newland, Sam, (4 October 1970), *Minneapolis Tribune*.

11. McCannel, Louise, (1967), The Way documents, Minnesota Historical Society.

12. Davis, Syl, (3 October 1970), The Way documents, Minnesota Historical Society.

13. The Way Board of directors, (16 December 1971), The Way documents, Minnesota Historical Society.

The Way and the Black Church

1. Gerlach, P. Luther and Hine, Virginia H., *People, Power, Change: Movements of Social Transformation*, (Indianapolis: Bobbs-Merrill, 1970), p. 24.

2. Ibid., p. 23.

3. Ibid., xviii.

4. Troeltsch, Ernest, "Sect-type and church-type contrasted." *The Social Teaching of the Christian Churches*, translated by Olive Wynn, (London: Allen and Unwin, 1951).

5. Caldwell, Angelia, painted a Black Christ at the Peoples Church. Photograph of author and painting (October 1970), *Hamline University Bulletin*.

6. Washington, Joseph, *Black Sects and Cults*, (New York: Doubleday Anchor Book, 1973), pp.131-132.

7. Gospel of Matthew 25:40, King James Version.

8. Davis, Syl, "On The Way From The Past To Our Future," (1984) Seventeenth Annual Board Meeting, Author's documents.

The Way and Black Power

1. El-Kati, Mahmoud, "The Definition Game," *The Way newsletter*, (20 September 1967), The Way documents, Minnesota Historical Society.

2. Edwards, Ron, *The Minneapolis Story Through My Eyes*, (Beacon on the Hill Press, Portland, Oregon, 2002), p. 205.

3. Boie, Maurine, *Study of Conflict and Accommodation in Negro-White Relations in Twin Cities*, (1932, Master Thesis, University of Minnesota), Minnesota Historical Society.

4. El-Kati, "A Way To Say It," (1967), Author's documents.

5. Gaye, Martin, (1967) AlbumTitle, *What is Goin' On.*

6. King, Dr. Martin Luther, "Vietnam and The Struggle For Human Rights," (4 April 1967), *Speeches About the War in Vietnam*, Annandale, Virginia: Turnpike Press.

7. King, Dr. Martin Luther, *Where Do We Go From Here? Community or Chaos*, (New York: Harper & Row, 1967), pp. 30-31.

8. Branch, Taylor, *Pillar of Fire*, (New York: Touchstone, Simon and Schuster, 1998), "Freedom Summer."

9. Cone, James H., *Martin & Malcolm & America: A Dream Or A Nightmare*, (New York, Orbis Books, 1991), pp. 231-232.

10. El-Kati, Mahmoud, "Way To Say It," (1967), op. cit.

11. El-Kati, Mahmoud, "The Role of the Negro in the Black Revolution,"(March 1968), Author's documents.

12. Carmichael, Stokely and Hamilton, Charles V., *Black Power*, (New York, Vintage Press, 1967), pp. 48-49.

13. Davis, Syl, "What Is The Way?" *The Way newsletter*, (21 June 1967), The Way documents, Minnesota Historical Society.

14. Douglas, Frederick, (1857), speech delivered at Canandaigua, New York, Author's documents.

FIVE: The Way Struggle Goes On: Creating the [Neighbor]Hood

1. Brueggemann, Walter, *The Covenanted Self*, (Minneapolis, Fortress Press, 1999), p. 77.

The Way Toward Inclusive Education: Antioch-Minneapolis Communiversity

1. Jones-Davis-Pyle, Gwyn, "Being Taught Not Caught," (1971), *Antioch-Minneapolis Communiversity Bulletin*, Author's documents.

2. El-Kati, Mahmoud, (1967), Special Education Program, Author's documents.

3. Ibid., pp. 2-3.

4. *Report of the National Advisory Commission on Civil Disorders*, commonly referred to after its chairperson, Illinois Governor Otto Kerner, (New York: Bantam Books, 1968).

5. Tillman, James A. and Mary Norman, "What Is Your Racism Quotient?" (1968, Privately Published)

6. Dewey, John, *Experience and Education*, (New York: Collier Books, 1966) p. 61.

7. Jones-Davis-Pyle, Gwyn, (1968), *University of The Way Bulletin*, Author's documents.

8. Freire, Paulo, *Pedagogy of the Oppressed*, (Harmondsworth: Penguin, 1972).

9. Berger, Peter L., *The Sacred Canopy*, (New York, Doubleday and Company, 1969), chapters 1 and 2.

10. Douglas, Frederick, (1857), speech delivered at Canandaigua, New York, Author's documents.

The Way Toward Restorative Justice:
Prison Rehabilitation Brought Home

1. Hand, Learned, *The Spirit of Liberty*, (New York: Alfred A. Knopf, 1953), p. 190.

2. "State's Prisons Rank Worst In Race Disparity," (8 June 1999), *Minneapolis Star Tribune*.

3. Southerland, Edwin, H., (5 February 1940), *American Sociological Review*.

4. Auden and Kronenberger, op. cit., p. 210.

5. "State's Prisons Rank Worst In Race Disparity," op. cit.

6. Edwards, op. cit., pp. 64-68.

7. West, Cornel, *Race Matters*, (New York: Vintage Press, 1993).

8. Edwards, *op. cit.*, pp.125-126.

9. Ibid., pp. 122-123.

10. Goffman, Irving, *Asylums*, (New York: Vintage Press, 1960).

11. Dixon, Willie Mae, (1967) Neighborhood Probationary Counseling Project, The Way documents, Minnesota Historical Society.

12. Brueggemann, Walter, *The Covenanted Self*, (1999), op. cit., chapter 6.

13. Gospel of Luke 19:1-10, Revised Standard Version.

14. Pranis, Kay, *Corrections Today*, (December 1997), pp. 74-75, 121-122.

The Way Toward Renewal Of Public Life:
Glenwood-Lyndale Redevelopment

1. Palmer, Parker J., *The Company of Strangers: Christians and the Renewal of America's Public Life,* (New York: Crossroads Publishing, 1983), p. 23.

2. El-Kai, Mahmoud, (1968), "Philosophy of Reform," Author's documents.

3. Sanders, Marian. K., *The Professional Radical: Conversations with Saul Alinsky,* (New York: Harper and Row, 1970), p. 33.

4. "Study is Scathing Indictment of Hollman Relocation," (10 August 2002), *Spokesman-Record.*

5. "The Promise in the North Side Renaissance: Housing for Everyone," Carrol Batsell Benner, Gregory Gray, and Matthew Ramadan (4 September 1999), *Minneapolis Star Tribune.*

6. Ibid.

7. Edwards, op. cit., p. 130.

8. Herron, Curtis, "If the City is Serious about Addressing Poverty," (6 September 1999), *Minneapolis Star Tribune.*

9. Ibid.

10. "Housing Settlement Misses its Mark," (4 February 2001), *Minneapolis Star Tribune.*

11. Edwards, op. cit., 135.

12. "If the City is Serious about Addressing Poverty," op cit.

13. "Housing Settlement Misses its Mark," op. cit.

14. "Closing the Gap is not only Right, it's Smart," (18 December 2005), *Minneapolis Star Tribune.*

15. "The Promise in the North Side Renaissance: Housing for Everyone," op. cit.

16. El-Kati, "Philosophy of Reform," (1968), op. cit.

The Way People Can Speak To Power:
Board of The Way and Greater Minneapolis Urban Coalition

1. Auden and Kronenberger, op. cit., p. 297.

2. "The Way," (1 December 1968), "Picture Magazine," *Minneapolis Tribune.*

3. Ibid., pp. 32-33.

4. Ibid., p. 33.

5. Ibid., p. 36.

6. Ibid., p. 36, 38.

7. Plank, Ray, Correspondence, (28 December 1967), The Way documents, Minnesota Historical Society.

8. The Way, op. cit., p. 36.

9. "Lincoln Slapping Incident II," (26 December 1967), *Minneapolis Tribune.*

10. "North Side Group Stresses Realism," (14 February 1968), *Minneapolis Star.*

11. Ibid.

12. Ibid.

13. Robinson, Rolland, Correspondence, (27 January 1968), The Way documents, Minnesota Historical Society.

14. Articles of Incorporation (1966), The Way documents, Minnesota Historical Society.

15. The Way Board press release (19 December 1967), The Way documents, Minnesota Historical Society.

16. Plank, Correspondence, op. cit.

17. Ibid.

18. Ibid.

19. Ibid.

20. Ibid.

21. Ibid.

22. The Way Board press release (2 January 1968), The Way documents, Minnesota Historical Society.

23. Davis, Syl, "Statement to the Urban League from Black Coalition," (9 July 1968), The Way documents, Minnesota Historical Society.

24. McCannel, Louise, Correspondence, (October 1969), The Way Documents, Minnesota Historical Society.

25. Harris, Larry and Williams, T., "Summary of a Statement of Action for an Urban Coalition," (December 1967), The Way Documents, Minnesota Historical Society.

26. Keating, Stephen F., "Urban Coalition Founding Document," (February 1968), p. 2, Author's documents.

27. Robinson, Rolland, (January 1968), "Urban Coalition and the Poor," The Way documents, Minnesota Historical Society.

28. McCannel, Louise, Correspondence, (April 1968), The Way documents, Minnesota Historical Society.

29. Ibid.

30. Wilderson, Dr. Frank, Press Release (16 November 1968), The Way documents, Minnesota Historical Society.

31. "Religion, Racism, and Paternalism," (17 November 1968), *Minneapolis Tribune.*

32. "Inner City Tensions Divide Sixty-year-old Congregation," (27 March 1970), *Minneapolis Star*.

33. "Social Action Pastor Backed," (28 May 1970), *Minneapolis Tribune.*

34. "Methodists Debate Future of City Church," (11 June 1970), *Minneapolis Star*. "'Peoples Church Stirs Debate at Methodist Parley," (11 June 1970), *Minneapolis Tribune*.

35. "Church's Activists Win Twice," (12 June 1970), *Minneapolis Star*. "Methodists Support North Side Church," (12 June 1970), *Minneapolis Tribune*.

36. Bowe, Jim, Correspondence, (15 July 1969), The Way documents, Minnesota Historical Society.

SIX: On My Way:
Coming Full Circle

1. Robinson, Rolland, *For A Moment We Had The Way*, (Expert Publishing, Inc., 2006), p. 198

On My Way From the Past to Our Future

1   Robinson, op. cit., p. 126

SEVEN: Appendices

Appendix I
The Way Programs:1966-1967

1. *The Way Newspaper*, (August 1968), The Way documents, Minnesota Historical Society.

2. The Way Board minutes (9 January 1969), The Way documents, Minnesota Historical Society.

Appendix II
The Way Programs:1968-1970

1. Way's Model For Developing and Demonstrating A Comprehensive Approach To Community Reform, (January 1970), The Way documents, Minnesota Historical Society, pp. 2-3.

2. Ibid., pp. 3-6.

3. Ibid., pp. 6-9.

4. Program Progress Report, (October 1969), The Way Documents, Minnesota Historical Society.

About the Author

Rolland Robinson is a United Methodist minister as well as a writer, playwright, and lecturer. Serving a church on the Near North Side of Minneapolis, Reverend Robinson joined Syl Davis in 1966 to offer leadership to **The Way.** He is presently serving a church in Taylors Falls, Minnesota. Since 9/11 he has lectured on "How Not To Become What We Hate" and "Truth Telling of Reconciliation: A Call to Repentance and Reparations." His most recent plays include *A Holy Terror* and *True Believers. A Holy Terror* is on the arrest and conviction of Jamil Abdullah Al-Amin, formerly known as H. Rap Brown. *True Believers* centers on the experiences and struggle of followers of Charles Manson. *For A Moment We Had The Way* is Dr. Robinson's first published book.